How Big? Dinosaurs

By Dougal Dixon and Patrick Corrigan

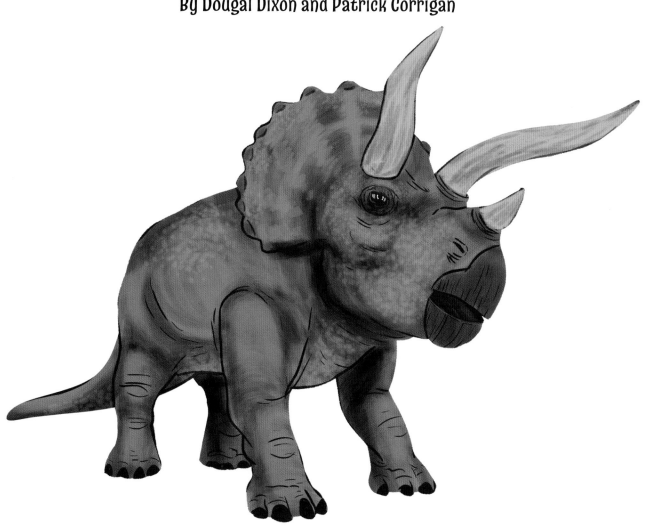

ARCTURUS

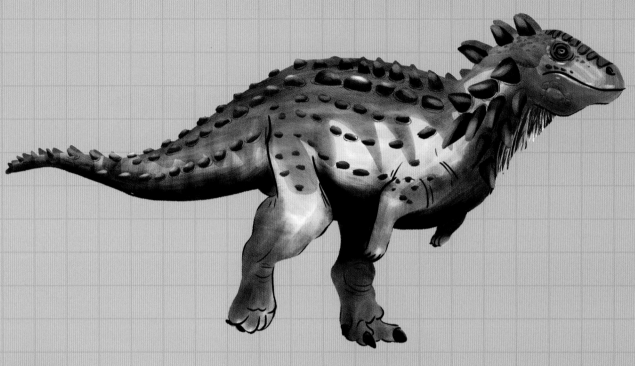

This edition published in 2024 by Arcturus Publishing Limited
26/27 Bickels Yard, 151–153 Bermondsey Street,
London SE1 3HA

Author: Dougal Dixon
Illustrator: Patrick Corrigan
Editor: Violet Peto
Designer: Simon Oliver
Managing Editor: Joe Harris
Design Manager: Rosie Bellwood-Moyler

ISBN: 978-1-3988-3622-8
CH011058NT
Supplier 29, Date 0224, PI 00003649
Printed in China

Contents

How Big?

When you think of the biggest land animals of all time, what comes to mind? If your answer is the dinosaurs, then you're right!

But just how big were they? This book will help you get the long and the short of a whole range of dinosaurs by giving you accurate measurements as well as real-life comparisons. We'll show you extraordinary details, like the toe bone that was so big that scientists thought it was a leg bone when they found it!

Size matters

How big was a *Tyrannosaurus* tooth? Or *Pendraig*'s footprint? This book *shows* you the actual sizes of dinosaurs and other prehistoric animals—or parts of them—on the page. You could also use a ruler to find out the exact measurements.

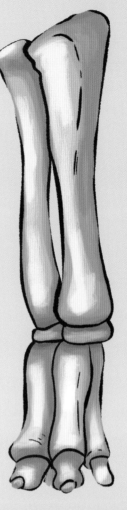

Length is measured in metric units (cm, m) or imperial units (in, ft). So we can say that *Stegoceras* was 1.7 m long, or we can say that it was 5.6 ft long.

Sometimes it's easier to picture how big something is by comparing it to other items. For example, we can say that a *Tyrannosaurus* tooth is about the same size as a banana.

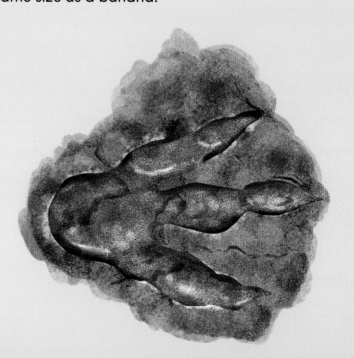

Weighing things up

Weight is measured in metric grams and kilograms (g, kg) or imperial ounces and pounds (oz, lb). You might say that *Velociraptor* weighed up to 15 kg or 33 lb.

It is not easy to estimate the weight of things that have been a long time dead. We only have fossils of their hard parts to go on.

Scientists must look at an animal's skeleton, and then figure out its weight based on how much muscle would be needed to make the skeleton move.

Scientists can also compare fossils to similar-sized modern animals and estimate the prehistoric animal's weight by comparison. So for example, the small dinosaur *Manidens* was about the size and weight of a modern raven, and a woolly mammoth was about the same size and weight as a modern Asiatic elephant.

Through the ages

Dinosaurs may have been the most spectacular animals of Earth's past, but they only lasted about 160 million years. There were other amazing animals that lived before, during, and after the Age of Dinosaurs, and we'll take a look at some of those, too. These include the extinct marine turtle *Archelon*, which was about as big as an inflatable boat!

How Big Was Anomalocaris?

If you were swimming in the warm sea of the Cambrian period—about 500 million years ago—you would have to watch out for this beast, which was the terror of the seas at the time.

Actual Size

This *Anomalocaris* fossil shows that a pair of long, grasping arms reached out from the front. These arms were probably used to pull in any small animal that it caught, bringing the prey into its mouth, where there was a ring of grinding teeth.

For a long time, scientists only found fossils of separate parts of *Anomalocaris*. For this reason, they thought that the jointed arm was a kind of shrimp, and the circular mouth with all its teeth was some kind of jellyfish.

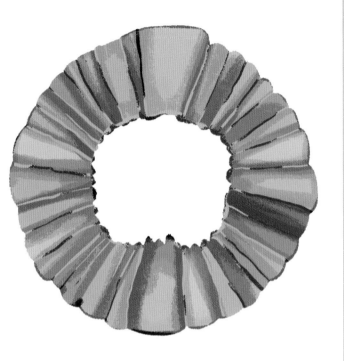

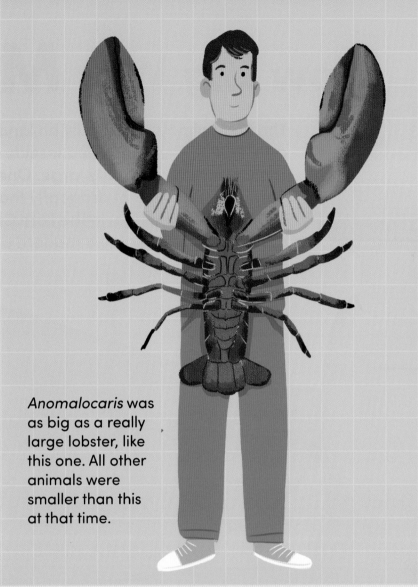

Anomalocaris was as big as a really large lobster, like this one. All other animals were smaller than this at that time.

It's no wonder that scientists had difficulty identifying the parts of *Anomalocaris*—all the animals back then were weird!

Hallucigenia, for example, with its many legs and spines on its back, was so strange that for a long time scientists did not know what way up it went, and which was the head and which the tail.

Opabinia was another odd animal. It had a long trunk with a grasping claw at the front, and no fewer than five eyes!

Both *Hallucigenia* and *Opabinia* were much smaller than *Anomalocaris*, at about the size of an adult thumb.

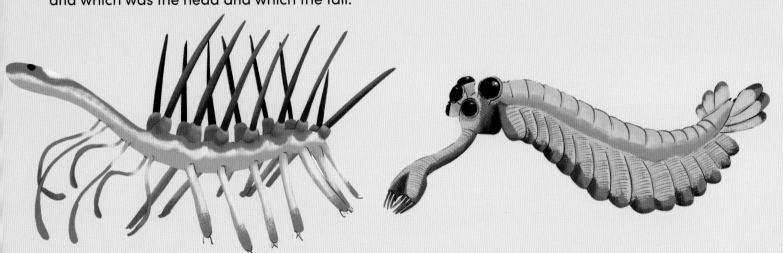

How Big Was **Meganeura?**

The first animals to live fully on land were arthropods. These included insects and spiders—some of which grew very large. One of these was *Meganeura*, a kind of dragonfly that lived about 300 million years ago, in the Late Carboniferous period. It was as big as a modern parrot.

Actual Size

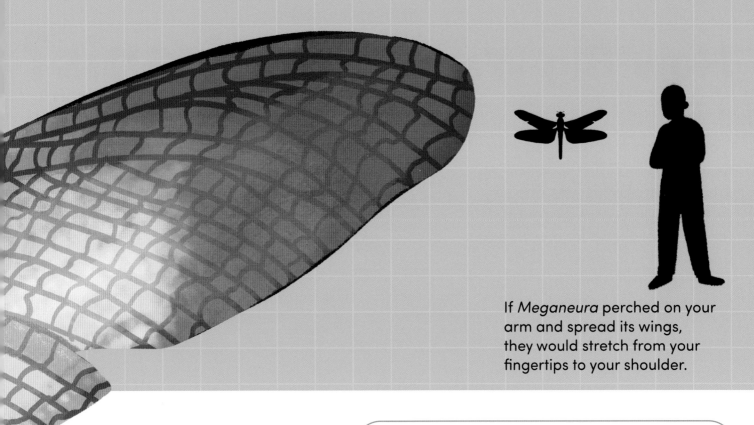

If *Meganeura* perched on your arm and spread its wings, they would stretch from your fingertips to your shoulder.

The earliest plants were small moss-like growths. Much later, they developed into trees, then thick forests. These forests provided a home for the early arthropods. *Meganeura* probably preferred open spaces with room to spread its great wings.

How do we compare?

	Female human	Meganeura
Weight	65 kg (143 lb)	150 g (0.33 lb)

Arthropleura was a massive millipede that lived at about the same time as *Meganeura* and was as long as you are! There was much more oxygen in the atmosphere at that time, which allowed giant arthropods such as *Meganeura* and *Arthropleura* to develop.

How Big Was Cephalaspis?

Our ancestors 400 million years ago were small fish that had no jaws. *Cephalaspis* was one of these. It had a shield around its forequarters, and its mouth was underneath. It spent its time sucking up food material from the sea bed.

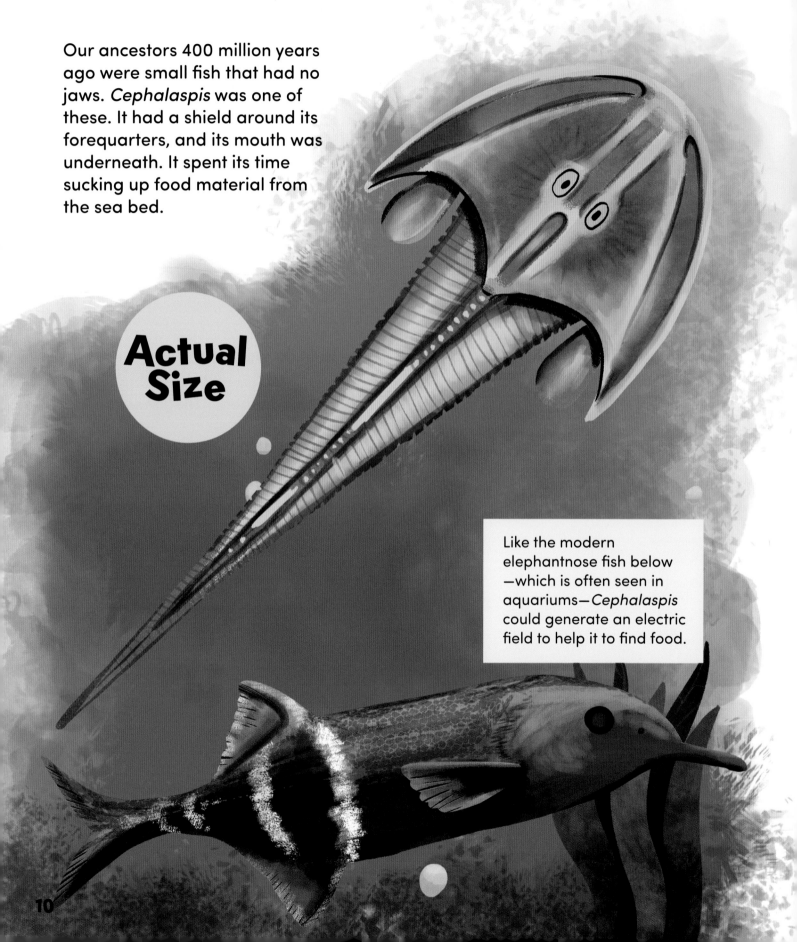

Actual Size

Like the modern elephantnose fish below —which is often seen in aquariums—*Cephalaspis* could generate an electric field to help it to find food.

Not all the fish 400 million years ago (in the Devonian period) were small. *Dunkleosteus* was as big as a shark, with massive jaws. Like *Cephalaspis,* it also had a shield around its head.

It is no wonder that the fish of the time were protected by shields! The fiercest hunters of the sea were the eurypterids, like this *Jaekelopterus*. These were giant sea scorpions, some of which were bigger than a grown man. They used their huge crab-like pincers to catch anything that swam.

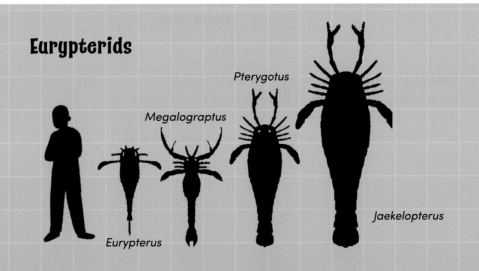

Eurypterids

Megalograptus

Pterygotus

Jaekelopterus

Eurypterus

How Small Was Westlothiana?

Among the first animals to live fully on land were small lizard-like reptiles, including *Westlothiana*. It lived in West Lothian, in Scotland, UK in the Early Carboniferous period, about 350 million years ago.

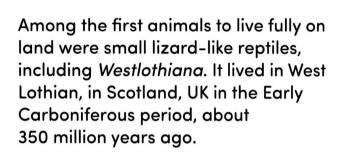

Actual Size

Westlothiana was the shape and size of a modern gecko and measured about 20 cm (8 in) in length.

It had a long tail, a slender body, and short legs. The relative length of the toes ensured that at least four of them were on the ground as the leg was swept back as it walked. It scampered about in the undergrowth of the ferny forests, feeding on other small animals that lived at the same time.

The lizard shape of the earliest land-living vertebrates was a good one. In fact, the shape was so successful that it is still widely seen today. All other land-living vertebrates developed from this simple plan.

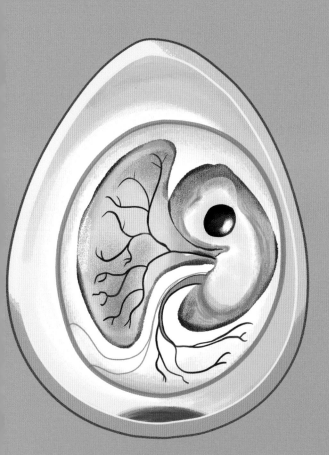

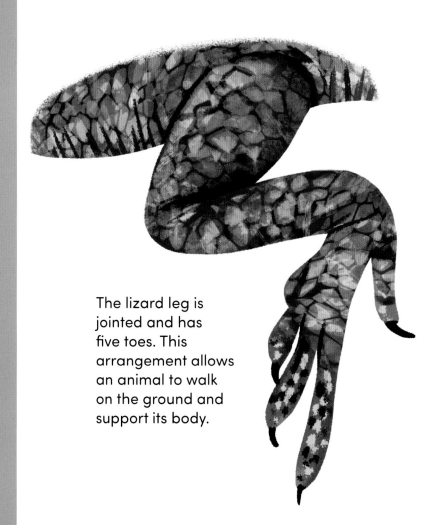

The lizard leg is jointed and has five toes. This arrangement allows an animal to walk on the ground and support its body.

Before the reptiles came along, all land-living vertebrates had to return to the water to lay their eggs and develop their young. In a reptile egg, the growing baby is surrounded by layers of membrane and shell. This is in effect a private pond in which the young can grow safely.

Like the modern gecko shown here, *Westlothiana* could have been held in your outstretched hand.

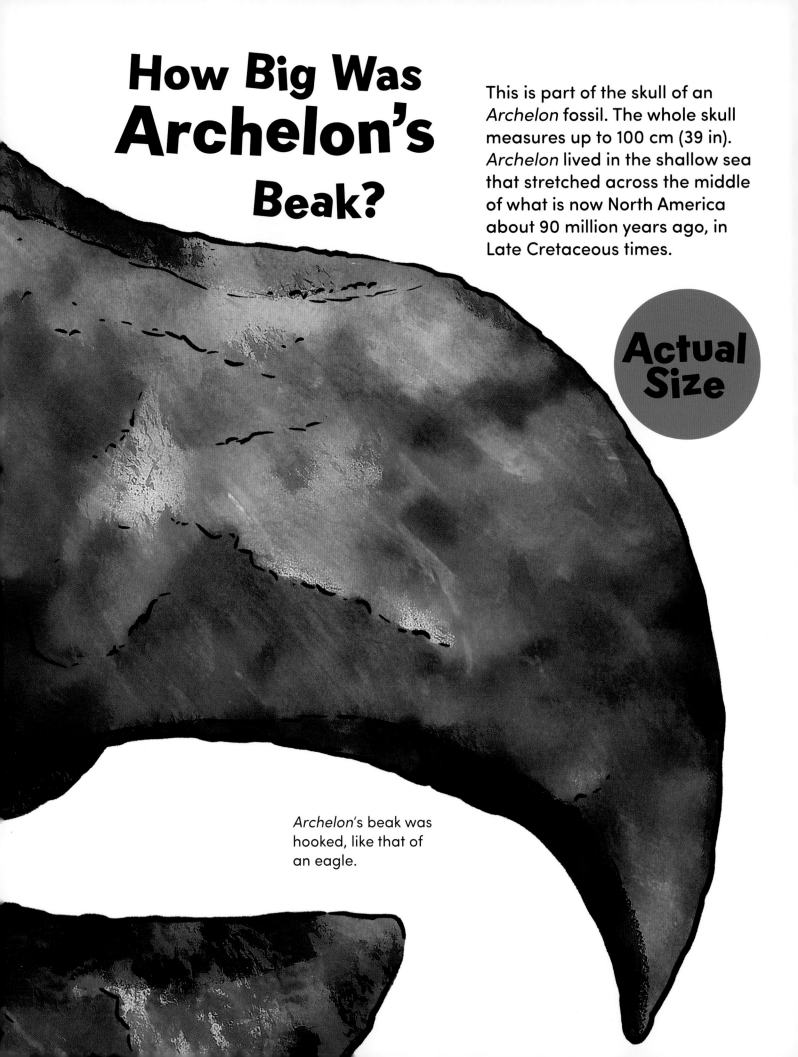

How Big Was Archelon's Beak?

This is part of the skull of an *Archelon* fossil. The whole skull measures up to 100 cm (39 in). *Archelon* lived in the shallow sea that stretched across the middle of what is now North America about 90 million years ago, in Late Cretaceous times.

Actual Size

Archelon's beak was hooked, like that of an eagle.

The beak of *Archelon* was covered in a horny sheath—just like the beak of a modern bird of prey. Scientists are not sure what it ate with this fierce beak, but it probably attacked large fish and swimming reptiles. Another idea is that it used its beak to break into the shells of the big shellfish that lived on the sea beds.

Archelon was as big as an inflatable boat.

How do we compare?

	Female human	Archelon
Weight	65 kg (143 lb)	2.22 tonnes (3.5 tons)
Length	1.7 m (5.6 ft)	4.6 m (15 ft)

Archelon did not have a solid shell. Its back was ridged with spreading ribs, and these had a leathery covering, like a modern leatherback turtle (see left).

How Big Were Atopodentatus' Teeth?

Many different kinds of animals went back to the sea after a period of living on land. Usually this was because there was plenty of food in the sea, and sometimes this was easier to find than food on land. *Atopodentatus*, which lived about 240 million years ago, was one of these.

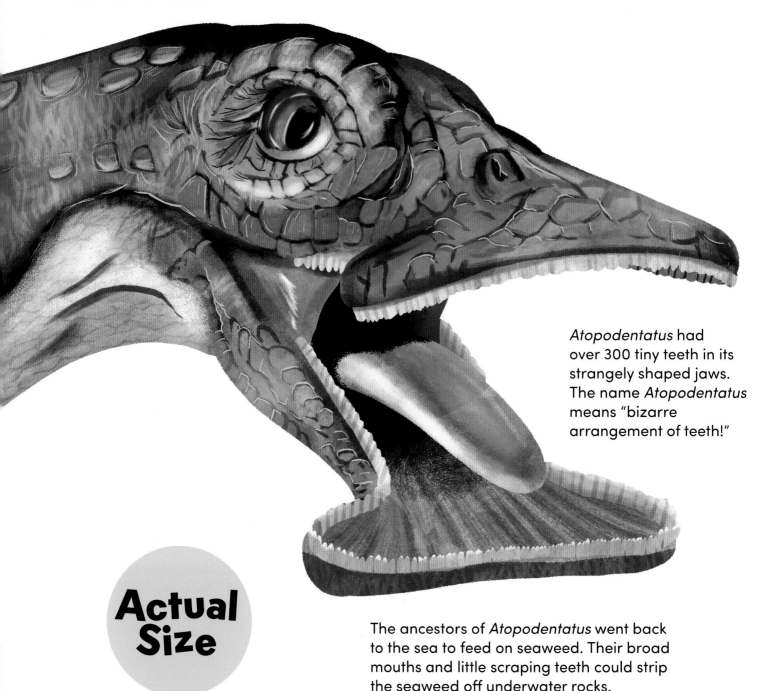

Atopodentatus had over 300 tiny teeth in its strangely shaped jaws. The name *Atopodentatus* means "bizarre arrangement of teeth!"

Actual Size

The ancestors of *Atopodentatus* went back to the sea to feed on seaweed. Their broad mouths and little scraping teeth could strip the seaweed off underwater rocks.

The body, legs, and tail of *Atopodentatus* were similar to the smaller-sized modern marine iguana (top right). The marine iguana has the same lifestyle, too—scraping seaweed from rocks in shallow water. But *Atopodentatus* lived 240 million years ago (in the Triassic period).

How do we compare?

	Female human	Atopodentatus
Length	1.7 m (5.6 ft)	2.75 m (9 ft)

The limbs of *Atopodentatus* were used for both swimming and walking on land, where it would sunbathe and build up strength for its underwater feeding trips.

How Big Was an Ophthalmosaurus' Eye?

Of all the reptiles that returned to the sea, the ichthyosaurs did it most perfectly. They became fish-shaped, with streamlined bodies, tail fins, and limbs converted to paddles. The first were small and seal-sized, then in Triassic times they became huge and whale-sized. In the Early Cretaceous period, they became quite small again—about dolphin-sized.

Ophthalmosaurus was a big ichthyosaur from 150 million years ago, in the Late Jurassic period. It hunted fish in deep waters, and needed big eyes to see its way around in the dark depths.

Actual Size

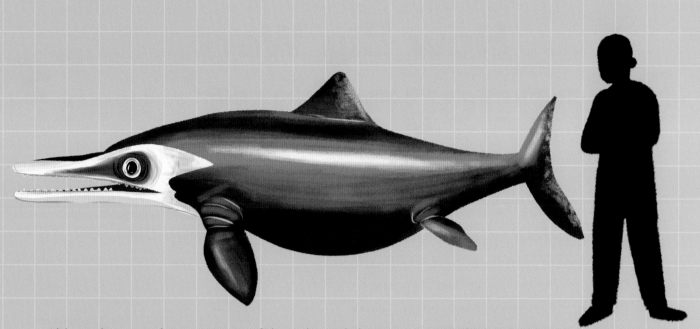

Although not as big as some of the other ichthyosaurs, *Ophthalmosaurus* still reached the size of a large dolphin. Its eyes were about the same size as those of a modern giant squid. They were used for the same purpose— seeing in the dark.

The eye of a big *Ophthalmosaurus* could be 23 cm (9 in) in diameter and was supported inside by a ring of bones.

How do we compare?

	Female human	Ophthalmosaurus
Length	1.7 m (5.6 ft)	4 m (13 ft)

Fossil of an *Ophthalmosaurus* eye

We know a lot about ichthyosaurs because of the number of fossils that have been found. Animals that live in the sea are more likely to become fossils than animals on land. Aquatic animals sink to the bottom and become covered in sediment that later turns to rock. An animal that dies on land usually rots away.

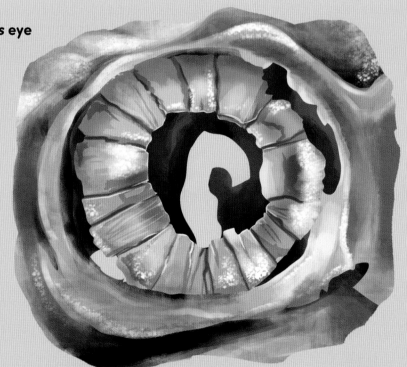

How Big Were Balaenognathus' Jaws?

By the time the dinosaurs evolved, other reptiles had taken to the skies. The pterosaurs were the flying reptiles of the Triassic, Jurassic, and Cretaceous times. They all flew with wings made of skin attached to a long, strong fourth finger. Some of these flying reptiles were as small as modern sparrows, while some reached the size of an aircraft.

There were dozens of species of pterosaur, each one adapted to foraging and eating a different kind of food. *Balaenognathus* lived about 150 million years ago, in the Late Jurassic, and filtered tiny animals from ponds and streams using hundreds of needle-shaped teeth with hooped tips.

Actual Size

The bottom jaw was curved upward and there were no teeth at the end of *Balaenognathus'* mouth, which flared out. This made it easier for it to scoop up mouthfuls of water containing small shrimp and other food. It would then squeeze out excess water through the teeth, leaving the prey intact inside the mouth, ready to be swallowed.

The jaws of *Balaenognathus* were similar to the bill of a spoonbill—a modern bird of about the same size, shown on the left.

Both the pterosaur and the bird waded in shallow water, dipping their long snouts under the surface and sifting out tiny animals.

Different pterosaurs had different diets—just like different birds have nowadays. We can tell that by the shapes of their jaws.

FISH-EATER   MEAT-EATER   FRUIT-EATER

Pterosaur

Pteranodon

Dimorphodon

Sinopterus

Modern bird

gannet

eagle

toucan

How Big Was Megalancosaurus?

The trees of Triassic times, 210 million years ago, were full of insects. Feeding on the insects were lizard-like creatures called the drepanosaurs. *Megalancosaurus* was one of these. It was about the same size as a modern chameleon.

Actual Size

It is not known exactly what the skin of the *Megalancosaurus* would have looked like.

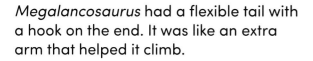

Megalancosaurus had a flexible tail with a hook on the end. It was like an extra arm that helped it climb.

The hump on the back held strong neck muscles. *Megalancosaurus* was able to dart its head about quickly to catch swift insects. Its eyes pointed forward to focus on its small prey.

How does it compare?

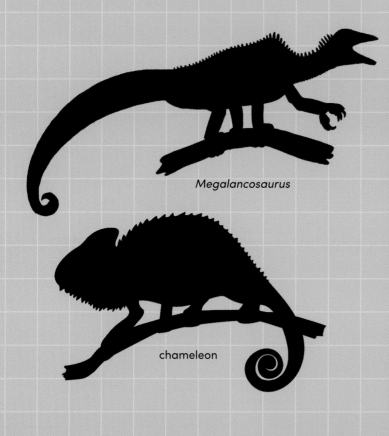

Megalancosaurus

chameleon

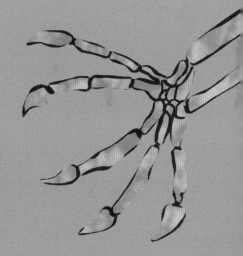

Like a modern chameleon, *Megalancosaurus* lived on the branches of trees. Its feet had three toes curving one way and two curving the other, allowing *Megalancosaurus* to perch in trees and grasp twigs.

How Big Was Coelurosauravus?

In the Triassic period, 250–200 million years ago, all sorts of reptiles took to the skies. They developed gliding wings, like parachutes, from flaps of skin along the sides of their bodies. They were very lightweight, and would have glided like paper darts.

Actual Size

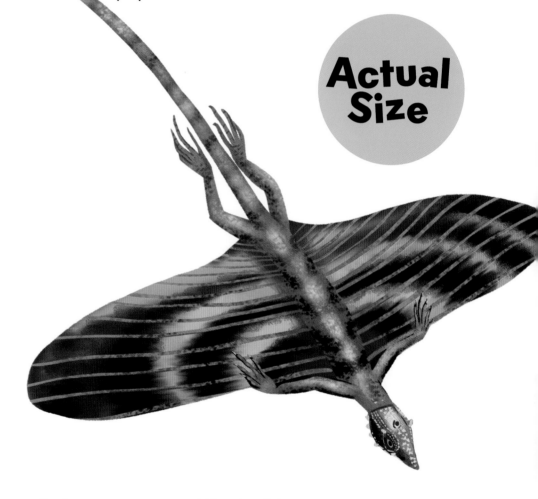

Coelurosauravus was a Triassic glider. Its wings were supported by fish-fin-like outgrowths from the ribs. When not airborne, *Coelurosauravus* lived in the branches of trees.

Pterosaurs, by contrast, were not just gliders. They were capable of powered flight because they could propel themselves through the air by flapping their wings. Pterosaurs were the most successful of the airborne reptiles, and flourished until the end of the Age of Dinosaurs.

Another glider, *Hypuronector*, had a deep fin on its tail to help it to steer.

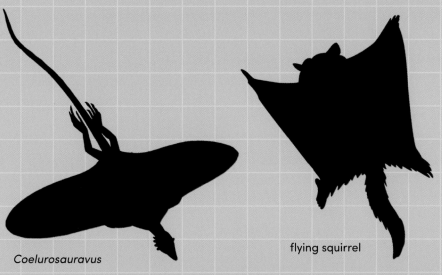

Coelurosauravus

flying squirrel

How does it compare?

A modern flying squirrel is about the same size as the Triassic gliding reptiles. It also glides on "wings" of skin, as they did.

How Big Was a Pterosaur Egg?

Until recently, scientists did not know what pterosaur eggs and babies were like. Then, in 2017, a huge area of fossilized pterosaur nests was discovered in China. It included hundreds of eggs, some of which contain partial embryonic remains of one species of pterosaur, *Hamipterus*.

It is believed that about 120 million years ago (in the Early Cretaceous period), a rookery of *Hamipterus* nests by a lake was flooded and the eggs were buried in mud in the lake, where they fossilized.

Actual Size

How do we compare?

	Female human	Hamipterus
Height	1.7 m (5.6 ft)	3.5 m (11 ft)

The eggs were found in several different layers in the sediment. Scientists think this may mean that the pterosaurs returned to the same nesting site each year—just as turtles and birds do today—and some eggs were washed away at different times.

An adult *Hamipterus* ranged from the size of a modern gannet to the size of an albatross. It had a wingspan of up to 3.5 m (11.5 ft).

It had pointed teeth that interlocked when the jaws were shut, which means it probably ate meat and, in particular, fish and other aquatic prey.

The eggs of pterosaurs had leathery shells like those of snakes and lizards, rather than hard shells like those of birds. Like snakes and lizards, pterosaurs also likely buried their eggs.

The youngsters may have been able to fly as soon as they hatched, although scientists now think that perhaps they were looked after by the adults for a while.

How Tiny Were Yi Qi's Wings?

The tiny tree-living dinosaur *Yi qi* lived in what is now China about 160 million years ago, in the Late Jurassic period. It glided on flaps of skin supported by long fingers and an extra bone growing from its wrist. This made the flaps look like the wings of a bat.

Actual Size

The strange wings were made from membrane and allowed *Yi qi* to glide from branch to branch in the dense forests in which it lived.

Yi qi would not have had the strength in its arms to fly with a flapping motion, like that used by a pterosaur or, later, a bird.

Dinosaurs with this weird type of wing did not last long. It was another group of dinosaurs that succeeded in flying in the long term—and later evolved into modern birds.

How does it compare?

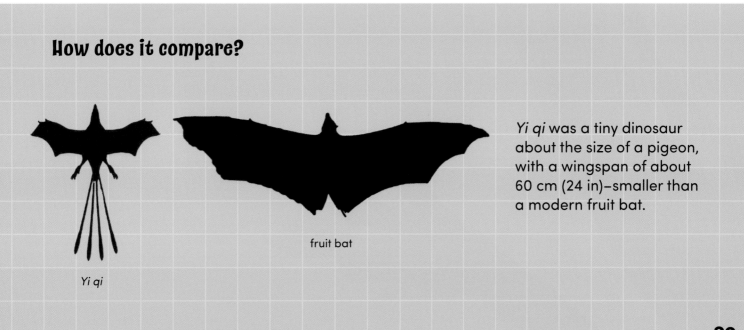

Yi qi was a tiny dinosaur about the size of a pigeon, with a wingspan of about 60 cm (24 in)—smaller than a modern fruit bat.

fruit bat

Yi qi

How Big Was Eoraptor?

Even dinosaurs started small! One of the earliest known types was *Eoraptor* from about 230 million years ago, in the Triassic period. It was only about 45 cm (1.5 ft) tall and 90 cm (3 ft) long—similar to a modern fox.

Its small size didn't mean it wasn't important, though. This little animal was the ancestor of many of the great meat-eating monsters and huge, long-necked plant-eaters that developed later.

Actual Size

Eoraptor was also a fast and fierce hunter, and tore its prey apart with its teeth and claws.

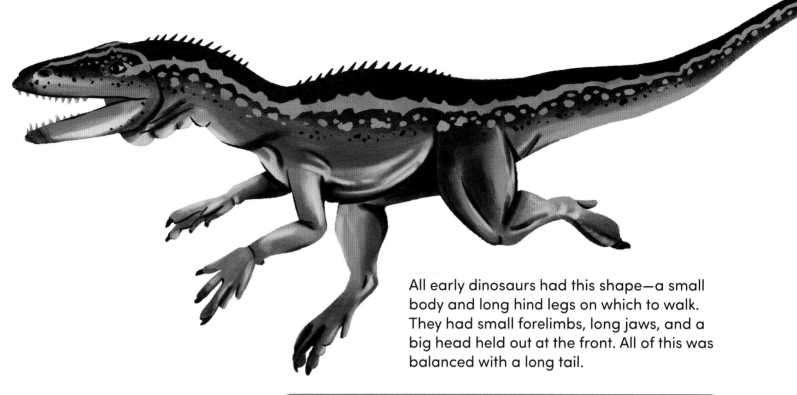

All early dinosaurs had this shape—a small body and long hind legs on which to walk. They had small forelimbs, long jaws, and a big head held out at the front. All of this was balanced with a long tail.

As well as being about the same size as a modern fox, *Eoraptor* lived in much the same way that a fox does—hunting small animals through the undergrowth.

How do we compare?

	Female human	Eoraptor
Weight	65 kg (143 lb)	10 kg (22 lb)
Length	1.7 m (5.6 ft)	0.9 m (3 ft)

How does it compare?

When we compare *Eoraptor* with the biggest of the plant-eating dinosaurs like *Brachiosaurus* and the biggest of the meat-eating dinosaurs like *Tyrannosaurus*, we can immediately see the vast range of sizes in the dinosaur group.

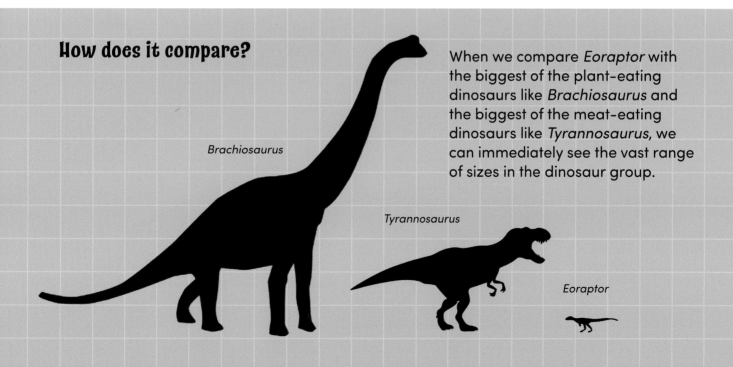

Brachiosaurus

Tyrannosaurus

Eoraptor

How Small Were Pelecanimimus' Teeth?

There were many types of meat-eating dinosaurs, and some became very much like ground-dwelling birds. *Pelecanimimus* was one of these. It belonged to a group called the ornithomimids—the "bird mimics"—and in many respects it resembled a pelican, hence its name.

Pelecanimimus lived about 125 million years ago, in the Early Cretaceous period, and its fossil was found in what is now Spain.

Actual Size

Most ornithomimids were toothless—like birds. But *Pelecanimimus* had about 200 tiny 5 mm (0.2 in)-long teeth.

Pelecanimimus lived in much the same way as a modern pelican, catching fish in shallow waters.

Most other ornithomimids were bigger than *Pelecanimimus*—usually about ostrich-sized. *Pelecanimimus* was earlier, too. It lived in the Early Cretaceous period, while its relatives were from the Late Cretaceous period, about 60 million years later.

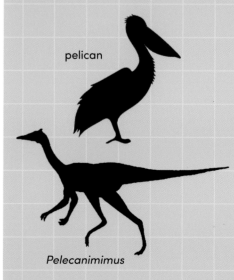

pelican

Pelecanimimus

How do we compare?

	Female human	Pelecanimimus
Weight	65 kg (143 lb)	30 kg (66 lb)
Height	1.7 m (5.6 ft)	1 m (3.3 ft)

How Big Was Incisivosaurus?

Actual Size

Imagine if your cat developed gnawing teeth at the front of its mouth and started eating leaves like a rabbit. This is the kind of surprise that met dinosaur scientists when they discovered *Incisivosaurus*!

Dating from about 125 million years ago, in the Cretaceous period, *Incisivosaurus* was a member of the meat-eating group of dinosaurs called the theropods, but it had plant-eaters' teeth.

Incisivosaurus was covered in feathers and had long feathers on its arms. This does not mean that it could fly. Most small dinosaurs were covered in feathers to keep warm.

The front teeth of *Incisivosaurus* were like those of a modern rabbit. They were used for gnawing. Along with its strong jaw muscles, it could gnaw away at tough plants.

How do we compare?

	Female human	Incisivosaurus
Weight	65 kg (143 lb)	30 kg (66 lb)
Height	1.7 m (5.6 ft)	1 m (3.3 ft)

How Big Was Saurornithoides?

If you saw *Saurornithoides* looking straight at you about 84–66 million years ago, in the Late Cretaceous period, you would be in trouble because this medium-sized, bird-like hunting dinosaur was an expert killer.

We can tell that because the eyes looked directly forward and were able to focus on whatever prey it was about to kill.

It was also a fast runner—the legs tell us that. So you would not have had much of a chance if you tried to run away!

What's more, it had a very large brain in relation to its body, so it was possibly pretty smart.

Actual Size

Once it had run down its victim, *Saurornithoides* would have killed it with a special big claw on its foot and torn it apart with its sharp teeth.

How do we compare?

	Female human	Saurornithoides
Weight	65 kg (143 lb)	52 kg (115 lb)
Height	1.7 m (5.6 ft)	Length 2.3 m (8 ft)

In body size, *Saurornithoides* was as big as a modern eagle owl. It had the same ability to look forward and focus on prey. The large eyes are evidence that it might have had very strong binocular vision.

How Huge Was an Alvarezsaurus' Claw?

Look at your hand—are there five fingers? That is the usual number of fingers and toes we find in vertebrates. However, most of the meat-eating dinosaurs had fewer fingers on their hands. Most had three but some had only two. And one group, the alvarezsaurids, had only one—and this bore an enormous claw.

Alvarezsaurus was a small meat-eating dinosaur that lived in the area that is now Argentina during the Late Cretaceous period, about 85 million years ago.

Actual Size

It had a long tail, and long, strong legs. The short arms had really strong bones, so the big claw on each arm must have had a lot of strength behind it.

The huge claws on a modern anteater are used for ripping into the solid clay of anthills and termite mounds. The claws of *Alvarezsaurus* and its relatives were probably used for the same purpose.

Alvarezsaurus

anteater

Alvarezsaurus would have eaten a lot of Cretaceous-period termites (below), which were very much like modern ones.

How do we compare?

	Female human	**Alvarezsaurus**
Weight	65 kg (143 lb)	3 kg (6.6 lb)
Height	1.7 m (5.6 ft)	1.4 m (4.6 ft)

How Big Were Masiakasaurus' Jaws?

This snaggle-toothed theropod from about 70 million years ago had strange teeth that protruded from the front of the jaws. These were ideal for catching and holding onto slippery, struggling fish.

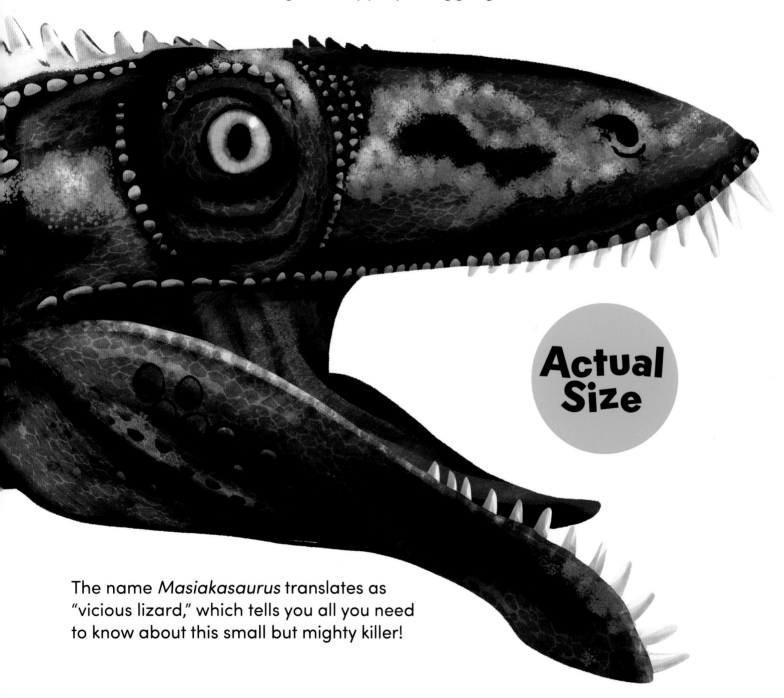

Actual Size

The name *Masiakasaurus* translates as "vicious lizard," which tells you all you need to know about this small but mighty killer!

In modern times, bears stand in rivers and catch fish swimming by. *Masiakasaurus* would have had the same feeding habits.

Lots of pointed teeth are a sign of a fish-eating animal. Look at today's fish-eating gharial—a crocodile with long, narrow jaws and many pointed teeth.

How do we compare?

	Female human	Masiakasaurus
Weight	65 kg (143 lb)	20 kg (44 lb)
Height	1.7 m (5.6 ft)	Length 2.1 m (6.9 ft)

How Big Was Oviraptor?

Found in Asia 85–75 million years ago, in the Late Cretaceous period, *Oviraptor* had a strange head for a theropod dinosaur, with short jaws, no teeth, and a beak. It was almost like the head of a bird. In fact, some scientists think it *was* a kind of bird.

So what could it have eaten? With those strong, curved jaws, something hard—maybe shellfish or the eggs of other dinosaurs.

Actual Size

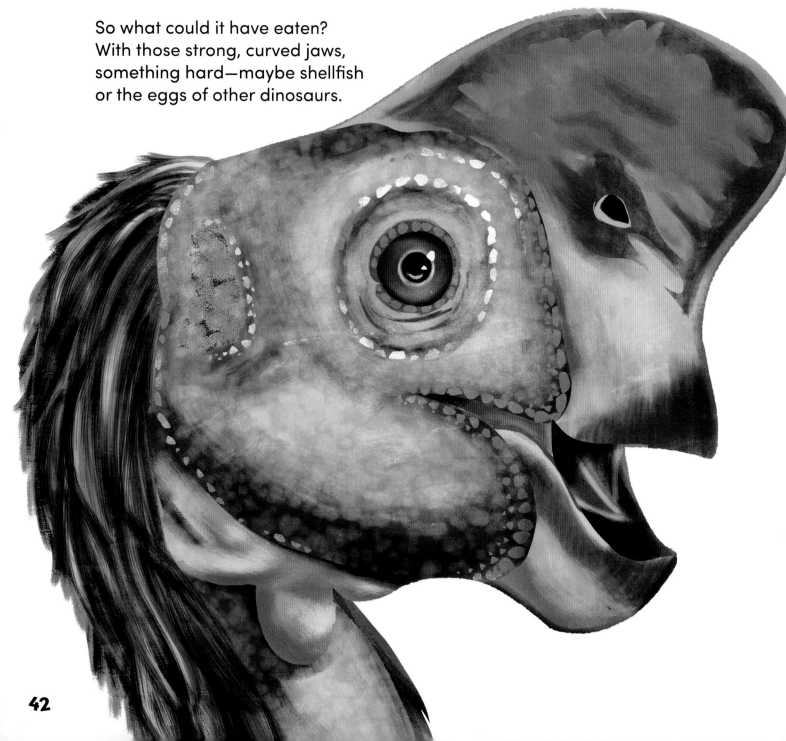

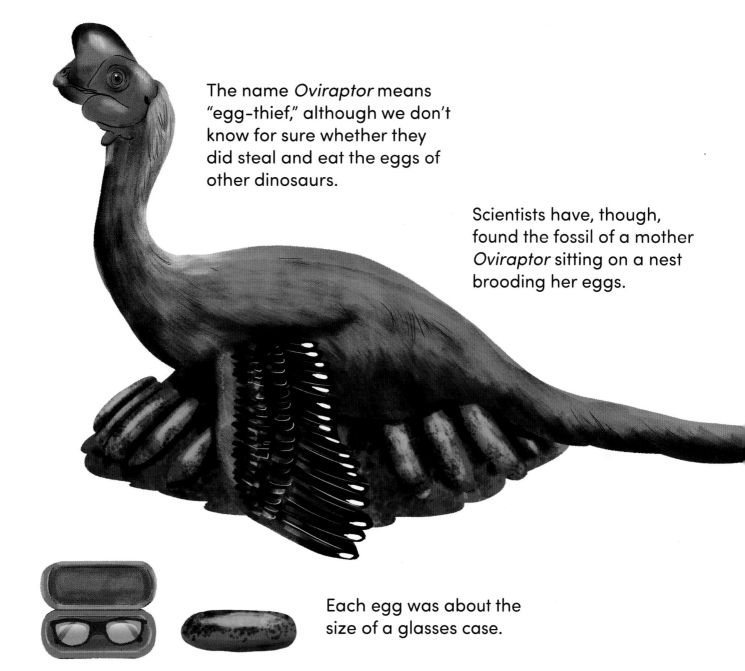

The name *Oviraptor* means "egg-thief," although we don't know for sure whether they did steal and eat the eggs of other dinosaurs.

Scientists have, though, found the fossil of a mother *Oviraptor* sitting on a nest brooding her eggs.

Each egg was about the size of a glasses case.

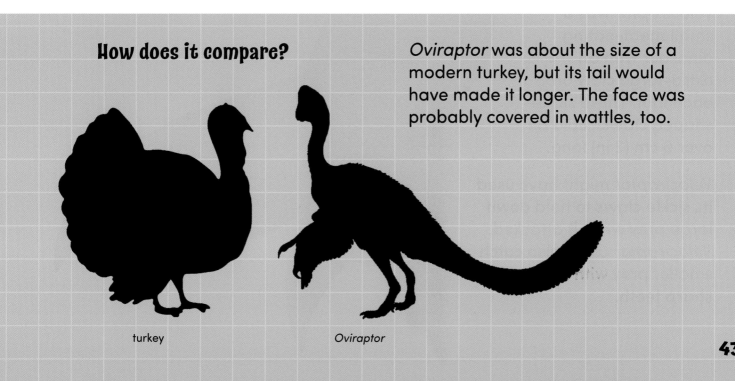

How does it compare?

Oviraptor was about the size of a modern turkey, but its tail would have made it longer. The face was probably covered in wattles, too.

turkey

Oviraptor

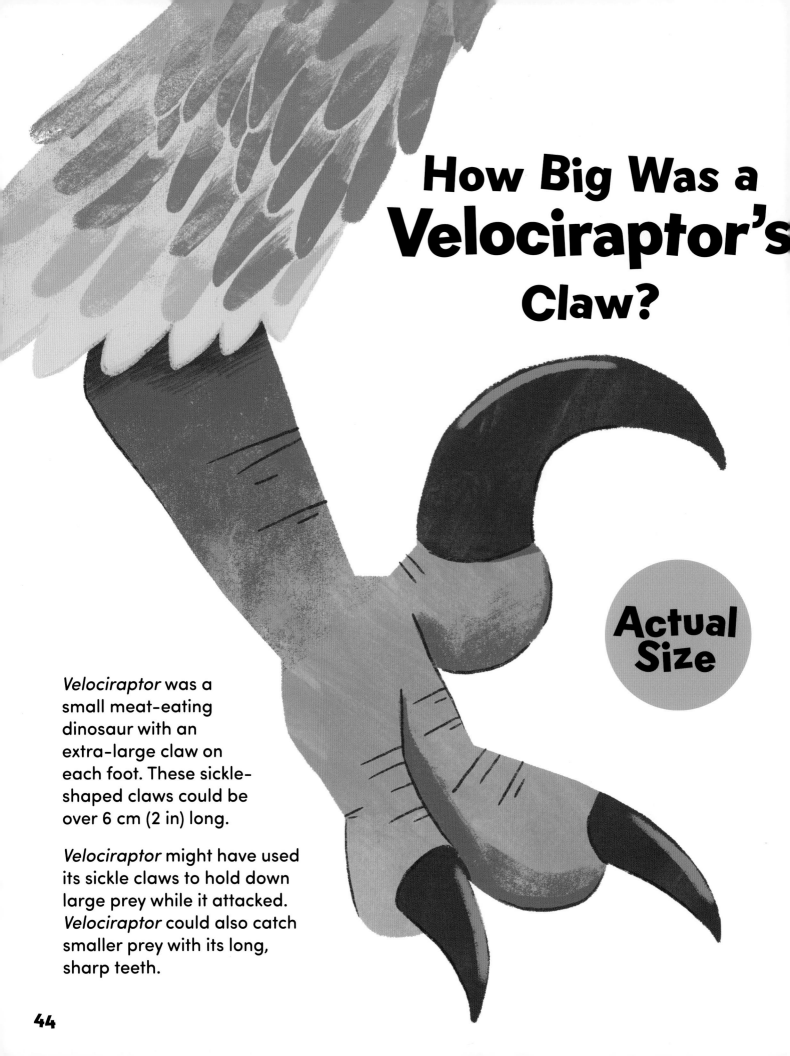

How Big Was a Velociraptor's Claw?

Actual Size

Velociraptor was a small meat-eating dinosaur with an extra-large claw on each foot. These sickle-shaped claws could be over 6 cm (2 in) long.

Velociraptor might have used its sickle claws to hold down large prey while it attacked. *Velociraptor* could also catch smaller prey with its long, sharp teeth.

While *Velociraptor* may have been small, it was a very effective hunter. It could run at over 60 km per hour (37 miles per hour), holding its sickle claws above the ground. That makes *Velociraptor* one of the fastest dinosaurs ever!

Velociraptor was about the same length as a wolf—around 1.8 m (6 ft) long.

Velociraptor couldn't fly, but it had feathers and wings. It might have used its feathery wings to protect its nest, to impress other creatures ... or to help it run even faster!

How do we compare?

	Female human	Velociraptor
Height	1.7 m (5.6 ft)	0.5 m (1.6 ft)
Weight	68 kg (143 lb)	15 kg (33 lb)

Velociraptor's tail made up half the length of its body. Its tail was up to 1 m (3.3 ft) long—about as long as a guitar.

How Huge Was a Tyrannosaurus' Tooth?

Including the root, a *Tyrannosaurs'* tooth could reach up to 30 cm (12 in) long. Only about 10 cm (4 in) would have been visible above the gum. Each tooth was the size, and rough shape, of a banana. But not as soft!

Actual Size

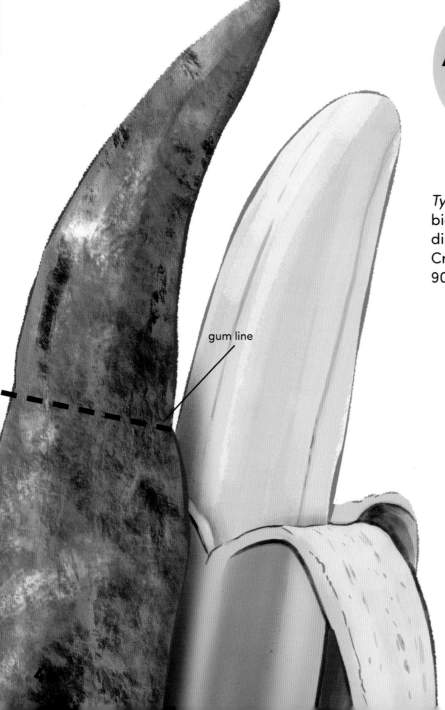

gum line

Tyrannosaurus was one of the biggest of the meat-eating dinosaurs at the end of the Cretaceous period, about 90–66 million years ago.

There were three kinds of teeth in the mighty jaws of *Tyrannosaurus*. Stout teeth at the front were for holding onto prey. Sharp teeth at the side were for shearing the meat, and bone-crushing teeth at the back were for pulverizing the skeleton.

This would have been the last thing many Late Cretaceous dinosaurs saw—the killing teeth of a *Tyrannosaurus*.

Based on fossil evidence, scientists think that *Tyrannosaurus* measured about 12 m (40 ft) in length and 3.7 m (12 ft) in height. It might have weighed in at a hefty 5,000–7,000 kg (11,000–15,500 lb)—about the weight of a large modern African elephant.

Tyrannosaurus had a heavy tail that was used as a counterweight to help it balance as it walked and ran.

How Big Was **Pendraig?**

We can tell a lot about a dinosaur from its footprint, such as how big it was and what family of dinosaur it belonged to. What we cannot tell, with certainty, is what particular dinosaur made the footprint!

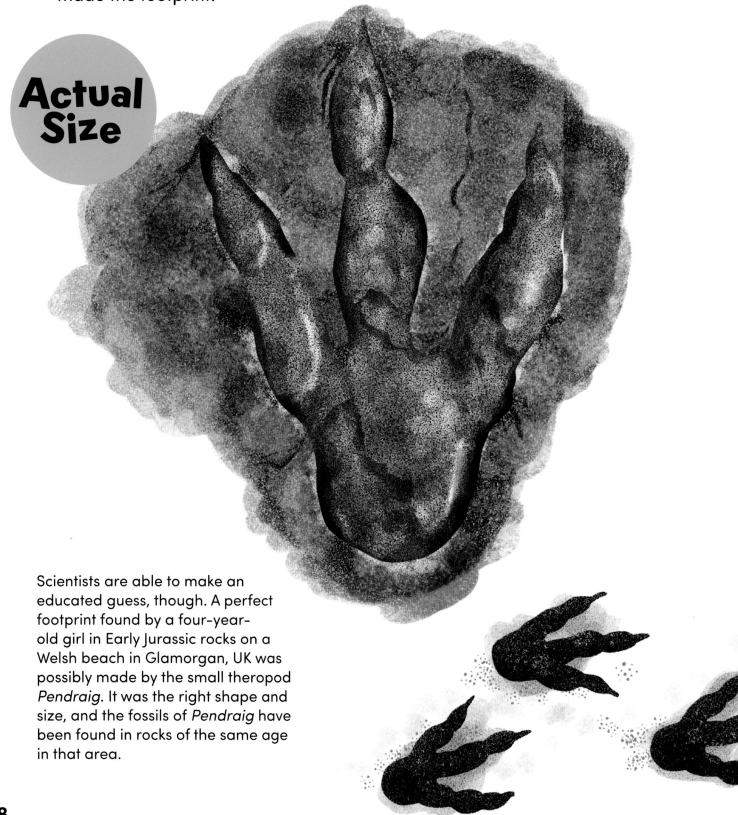

Actual Size

Scientists are able to make an educated guess, though. A perfect footprint found by a four-year-old girl in Early Jurassic rocks on a Welsh beach in Glamorgan, UK was possibly made by the small theropod *Pendraig*. It was the right shape and size, and the fossils of *Pendraig* have been found in rocks of the same age in that area.

48

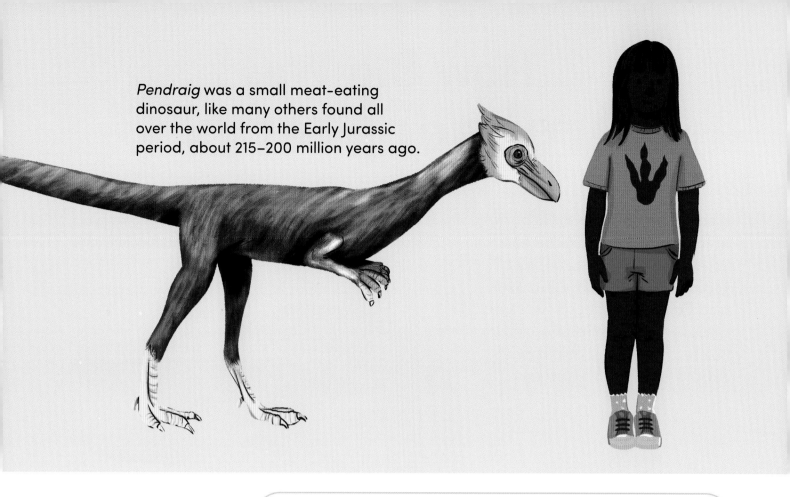

Pendraig was a small meat-eating dinosaur, like many others found all over the world from the Early Jurassic period, about 215–200 million years ago.

Finding a whole track of dinosaur footprints is more useful than finding one. Then we can tell how fast they walked and whether they lived in herds or roamed alone. We still cannot tell what particular dinosaur made those tracks, though.

How do we compare?

	Female human	Pendraig
Weight	65 kg (143 lb)	1.6 kg (3.5 lb)
Length	1.7 m (5.6 ft)	1.21 m (4 ft)

How Big Was Archaeopteryx?

Birds evolved from dinosaurs. In fact, technically, birds can be called dinosaurs. Many of the dinosaurs of Late Jurassic and Early Cretaceous times had a mixture of reptile and bird-like features. One of the best examples is *Archaeopteryx*.

The name *Archaeopteryx* means "ancient feather" or "ancient wing."

Archaeopteryx lived about 150 million years ago in the region that is now southern Germany.

Actual Size

Archaeopteryx had a reptile's tail, clawed fingers on the wings, and jaws full of teeth rather than a beak. Modern birds have none of these things.

But it was covered in feathers, and the flight feathers on the wings were arranged just like those of a modern bird.

We know all about *Archaeopteryx* because of the beautifully detailed fossils we have found.

How does it compare?

Archaeopteryx was the size of a modern raven.

Archaeopteryx

raven

How Big Was a Diplodocus' Tooth?

The biggest dinosaurs of all were the sauropods—huge plant-eaters with long necks and long tails. To feed such great bodies they needed special teeth to gather enough food. Those of *Diplodocus* were like the teeth of a comb, and they were used to rake the leaves and twigs from trees.

Diplodocus lived during the Late Jurassic period, about 155–145 million years ago. Its bones are often found in the same places as those of *Allosaurus* and *Stegosaurus*.

Actual Size

How do we compare?

	Female human	Diplodocus
Weight	65 kg (143 lb)	22,680 kg (25 tons)
Length	1.7 m (5.6 ft)	30 m (98 ft)

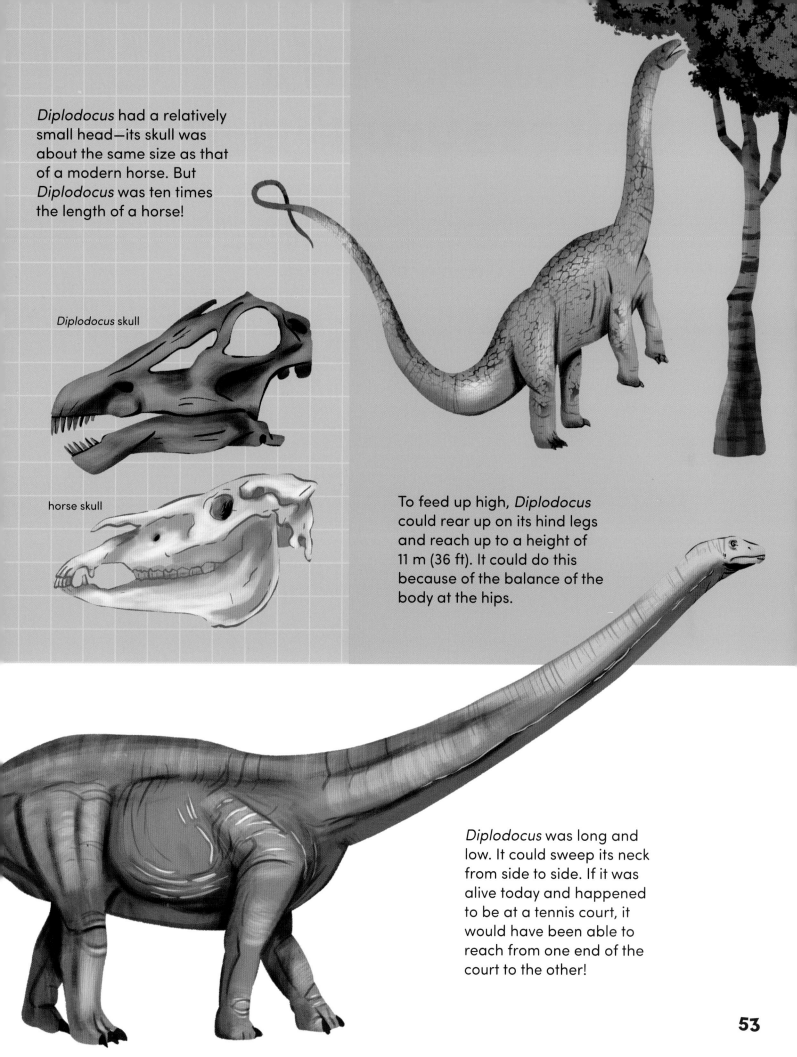

Diplodocus had a relatively small head—its skull was about the same size as that of a modern horse. But *Diplodocus* was ten times the length of a horse!

Diplodocus skull

horse skull

To feed up high, *Diplodocus* could rear up on its hind legs and reach up to a height of 11 m (36 ft). It could do this because of the balance of the body at the hips.

Diplodocus was long and low. It could sweep its neck from side to side. If it was alive today and happened to be at a tennis court, it would have been able to reach from one end of the court to the other!

How Big Was a
Saltasaurus' Egg?

Most dinosaurs did not hatch out of leathery-shelled eggs like pterosaurs and crocodiles. They had hard-shelled eggs like birds. We sometimes find them as fossils, but, like footprints, it is often difficult to tell which species of dinosaur laid which egg.

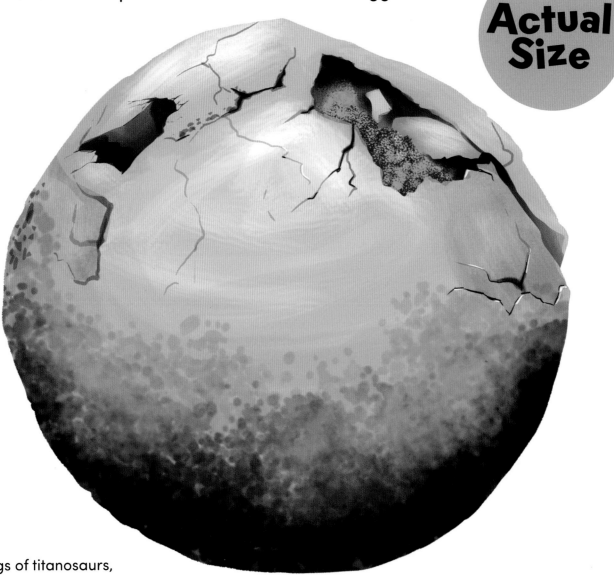

Actual Size

The eggs of titanosaurs, such as *Saltasaurus*, which lived about 70 million years ago, were only the size of ostrich eggs. If eggs were any bigger, the shell would be too thick and tough for the baby to hatch through it!

Scientists have found vast areas of nests in Argentina and India. But these were only part of the areas uncovered—there might be many more nests that are yet to be discovered.

How does it compare?

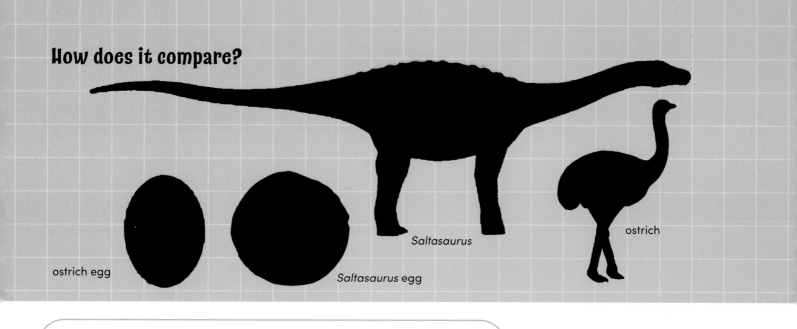

ostrich egg

Saltasaurus

Saltasaurus egg

ostrich

How do we compare?

	Female human	Saltasaurus
Weight	65 kg (143 lb)	2.5 tonnes (2.8 tons)
Length	1.7 m (5.6 ft)	8.5 m (28 ft)

We know that whole herds of the biggest dinosaurs—the sauropod group called the titanosaurs—laid their eggs together in herds.

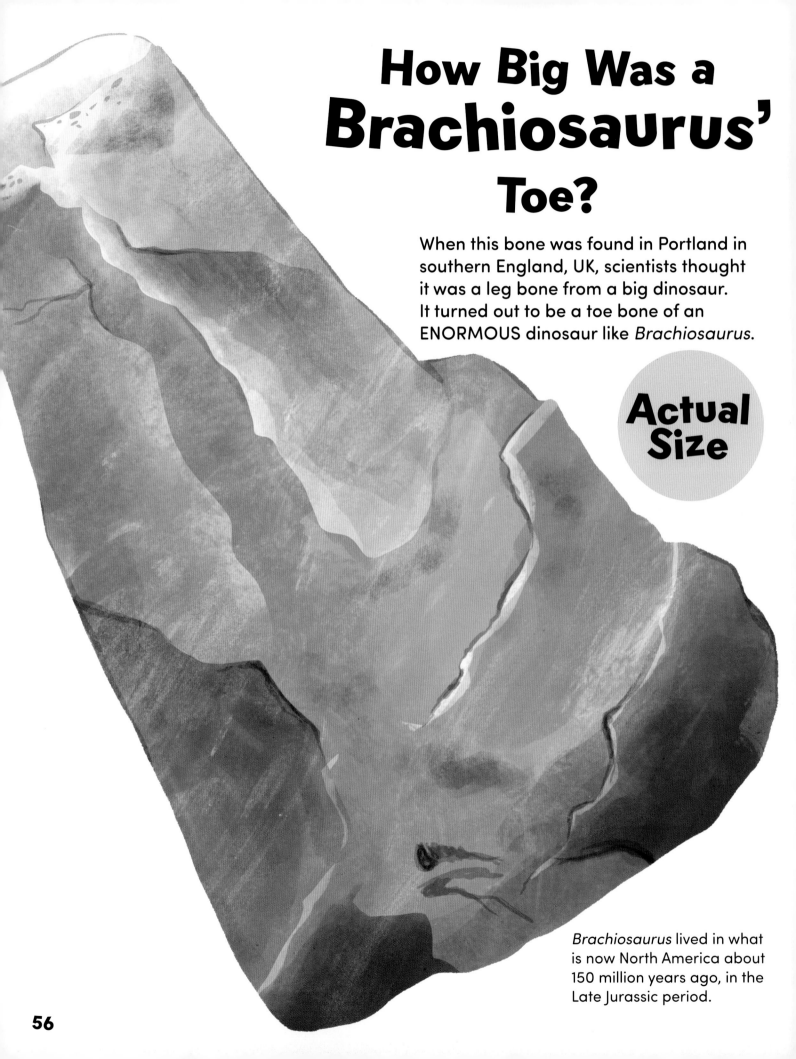

How Big Was a
Brachiosaurus' Toe?

When this bone was found in Portland in southern England, UK, scientists thought it was a leg bone from a big dinosaur. It turned out to be a toe bone of an ENORMOUS dinosaur like *Brachiosaurus*.

Actual Size

Brachiosaurus lived in what is now North America about 150 million years ago, in the Late Jurassic period.

The high shoulders meant that the head of *Brachiosaurus* could reach up into trees without it needing to stand up on its hind legs with its forelegs off the ground.

Brachiosaurus belonged to the same group of sauropods as the titanosaurs. It had very long arm bones compared to *Diplodocus*.

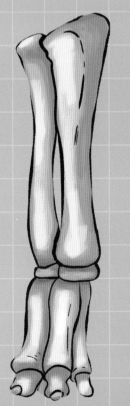

People often ask why some dinosaurs became so big. Wrong question! We should be asking why modern animals are not bigger. The main answer is that modern big animals are mammals and warm-blooded, which means they need a lot of energy from food. A warm-blooded mammal the size of *Brachiosaurus* would simply not be able to eat enough to generate enough energy to stay alive.

How do we compare?

	Female human	Brachiosaurus
Weight	65 kg (143 lb)	47 tonnes (52 tons)
Length	1.7 m (5.6 ft)	22 m (72ft)

How Big Was a Dinosaur Scute?

Some of the titanosaurs developed shields on their backs, either for protection or for stiffening the backbone. *Ampelosaurus* was one of these. It lived about 71 million years ago, during the Late Cretaceous period.

Actual Size

These scutes (lumps of skin and bone) belonged to an *Ampelosaurus*. They formed a layer that protected its backbone.

A lump of protective shield like this would have made the animal unappetizing for a meat-eating dinosaur.

The scutes were embedded in a mass of small bead-like scales that covered the whole animal.

The biggest of the scutes on the back of *Ampelosaurus* were about the size of dinner plates.

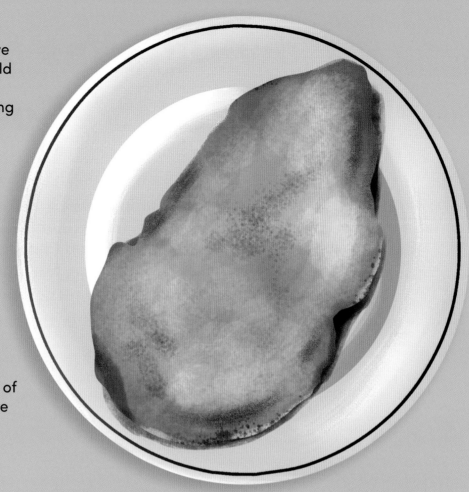

Different-shaped shields were embedded in the skin over different parts of the body. The animal was about the size of an elephant. Just imagine an elephant covered in protection like this!

How do we compare?

	Female human	Ampelosaurus
Weight	65 kg (143 lb)	8 tonnes (8.8 tons)
Length	1.7 m (5.6 ft)	16 m (52 ft)

As well as being for protection, the scutes would have been used for storing minerals. These would be needed as a dietary supplement during seasons when there wasn't much food.

How Big Was a Manidens' Foot?

Some of the small plant-eating dinosaurs may have been able to climb trees. They were certainly small and agile enough to do so, and there was plenty of food to be had among the leaves and twigs. Some, like little *Manidens*, even had toes that could grasp branches.

Manidens lived at the same time and in the same place as several fierce meat-eating dinosaurs, about 179 million years ago. Its ability to climb trees would have kept it safe from these dinosaurs.

Actual Size

Like modern perching birds, *Manidens* had long toe bones that could clutch onto branches, and a first toe that pointed backward.

Manidens was about the size of a modern raven. It is thought that it would have measured 60–75 cm (24–30 in) in length.

Manidens

raven

Manidens belongs to a group of dinosaurs called the heterodontosaurids. These had strong forelimbs and, unusually for dinosaurs, five fingers—a great help in climbing.

Cheek pouches at the side of the mouth, and the different types of teeth, show that *Manidens* could feed on leaves and fruits found in trees.

How Big Was Jakapil?

We usually imagine bony-plated dinosaurs as being big and heavy like a *Stegosaurus*. But *Jakapil*, which lived about 100 million years ago, was only the size of a cat.

Actual Size

That's where the similarity ends, though—*Jakapil* didn't look anything like a cat! Instead of fur, it was covered in bony plates and spikes. These would have helped to protect the dinosaur from predators.

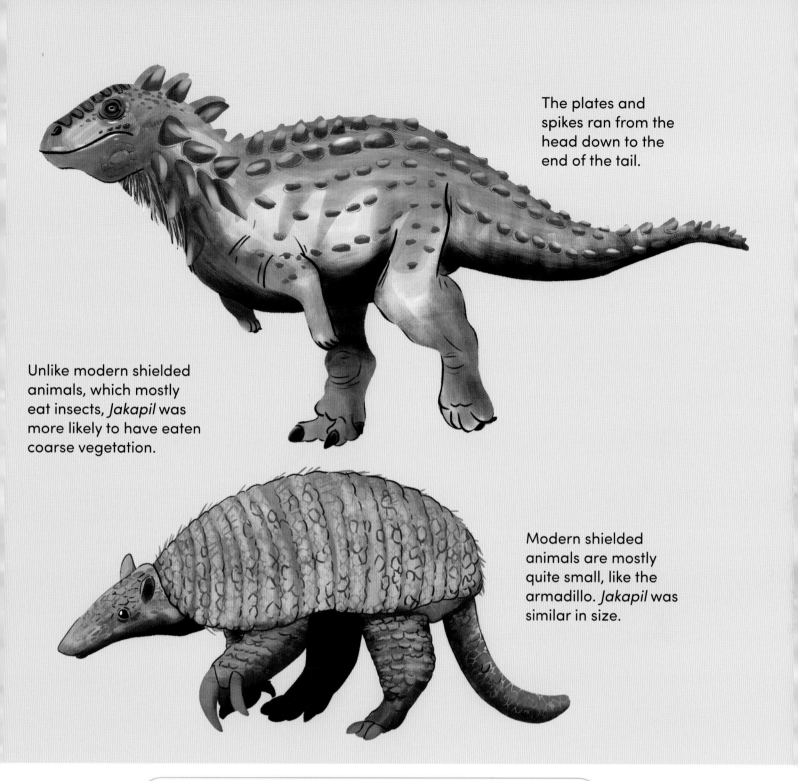

The plates and spikes ran from the head down to the end of the tail.

Unlike modern shielded animals, which mostly eat insects, *Jakapil* was more likely to have eaten coarse vegetation.

Modern shielded animals are mostly quite small, like the armadillo. *Jakapil* was similar in size.

How do we compare?

	Female human	Jakapil
Weight	65 kg (143 lb)	7 kg (15 lb)
Length	1.7 m (5.6 ft)	1.5 m (4.9 ft)

How Long Was a Stegosaurus' Tail Spike?

One of the most recognizable dinosaurs, *Stegosaurus* was a large, slow-moving plant-eater that lived about 150 million years ago, in the Late Jurassic period. It is best-known for its huge back plates and long tail spikes.

Although scientists are not sure exactly what the plates were for, it seems likely that *Stegosaurus* would have used the tail spikes to defend itself. This was handy, since it couldn't run very fast.

This is just a part of the tail weapon that was swung by an adult *Stegosaurus*. The whole spike would have been as long as your arm. And *Stegosaurus* had four spikes!

Actual Size

The point of the spike we see here is the bony core. In life, it would have been covered with a layer of horny skin—like the horn of a cow—that would have come to a sharp penetrating point.

How do we compare?

	Female human	Stegosaurus
Weight	65 kg (143 lb)	5.3 tonnes (5.8 tons)
Length	1.7 m (5.6 ft)	7 m (23 ft)

Stegosaurus not only had a spiky tail, it also had a double row of plates sticking up along its back. These may also have been used for protection, or for body temperature regulation or sending signals.

The spikes were about the size of a workman's pick. Imagine being struck by the point of one of those, having been swung with the full power of a *Stegosaurus*' tail!

The spikes were swung sideways at the legs and flanks of attacking meat-eaters.

How Big Was an Iguanodon's Hand?

Iguanodon was a big plant-eating dinosaur from 140–110 million years ago. It had a very large, very useful hand that could do lots of things. Its little finger, which was bigger than your entire hand, could curl over and act as a thumb.

Actual Size

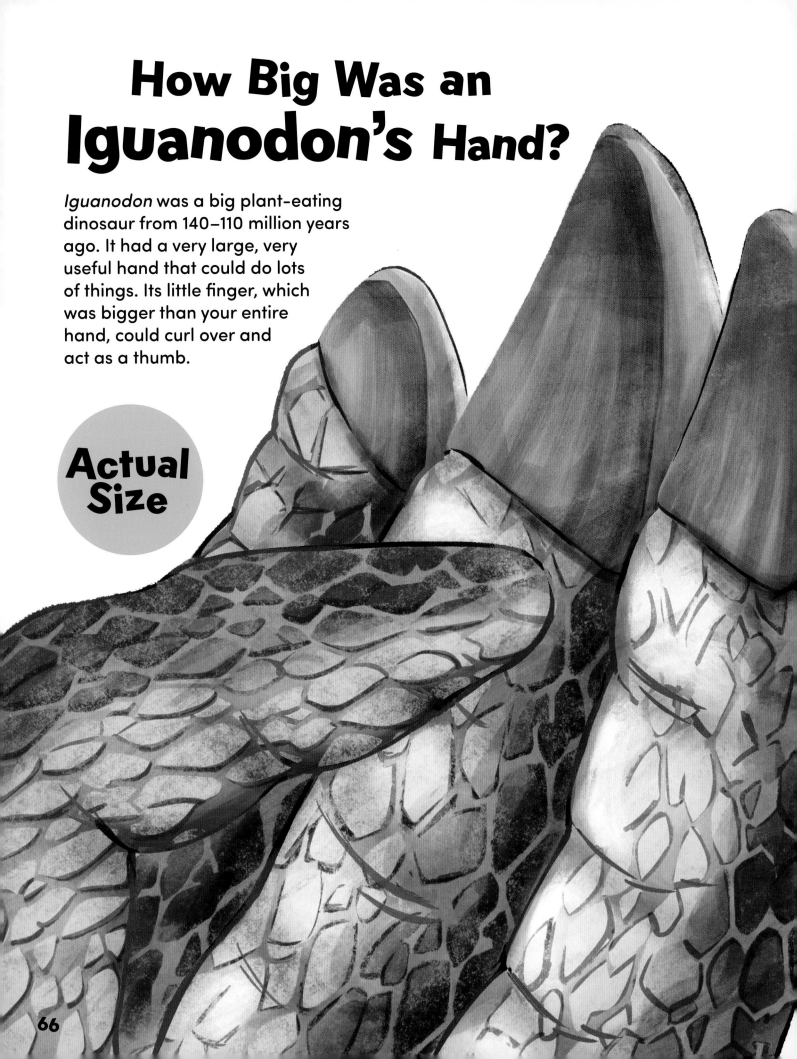

The first finger, where our thumb would be, was a solid spike. This was used as a weapon or for tearing down tree branches.

The middle three fingers were strong and had hooves at the end. These supported the front of the animal when it walked on four limbs.

The fifth, or little, finger could be used to grasp food.

Bigger than an elephant, *Iguanodon* needed the strong middle fingers to help support its great weight. It measured about 9 m (30 ft) long and stood nearly 2 m (6.6 ft) at the hip.

How Big Was an Ouranosaurus' Thumb?

Like its close relative *Iguanodon*, *Ouranosaurus* had a thumb spike it used for fighting or gathering food.

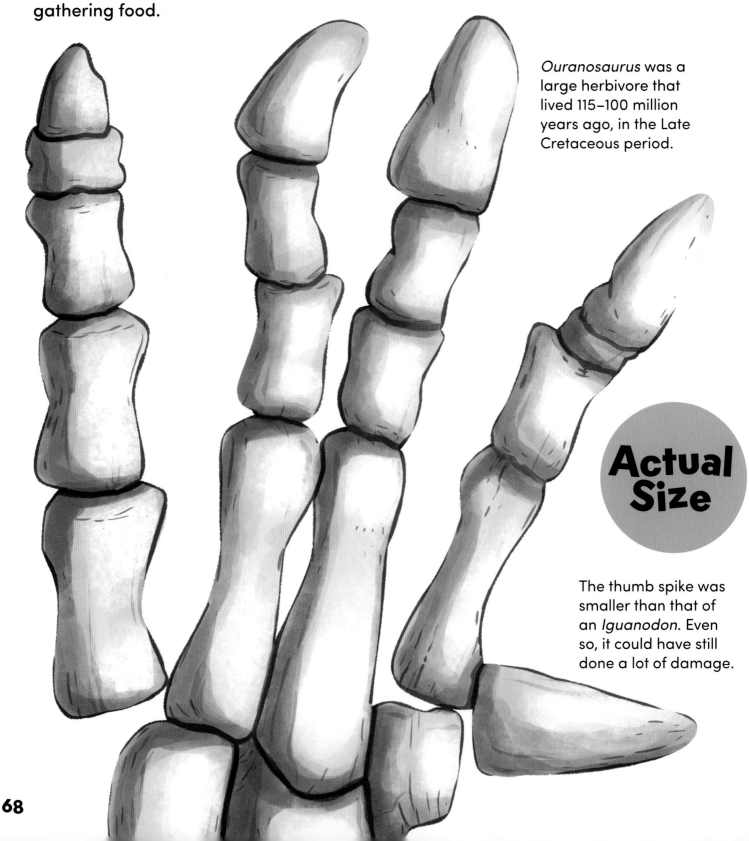

Ouranosaurus was a large herbivore that lived 115–100 million years ago, in the Late Cretaceous period.

Actual Size

The thumb spike was smaller than that of an *Iguanodon*. Even so, it could have still done a lot of damage.

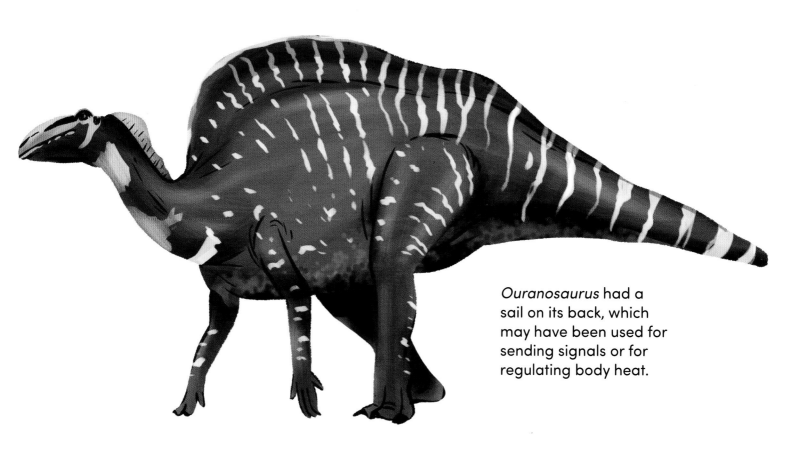

Ouranosaurus had a sail on its back, which may have been used for sending signals or for regulating body heat.

There were other animals with sails in ancient times.

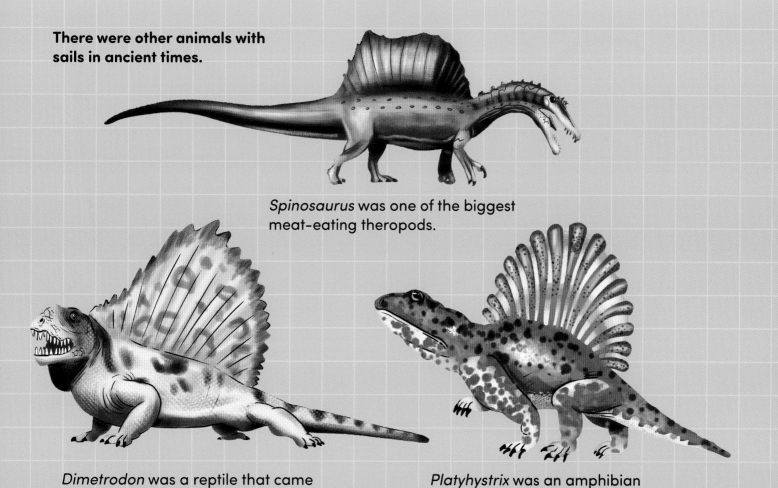

Spinosaurus was one of the biggest meat-eating theropods.

Dimetrodon was a reptile that came long before the dinosaurs.

Platyhystrix was an amphibian that came before all of them.

How Big Was a Lambeosaurus' Crest?

Close relatives of *Iguanodon* were the duckbills—so called because of their broad, duck-like beaks. Many of these, such as *Lambeosaurus*—which came after *Iguanodon* and lived about 75 million years ago—had tall crests on their heads.

Actual Size

A *Lambeosaurus'* crest was about 30 cm (12 in) tall.

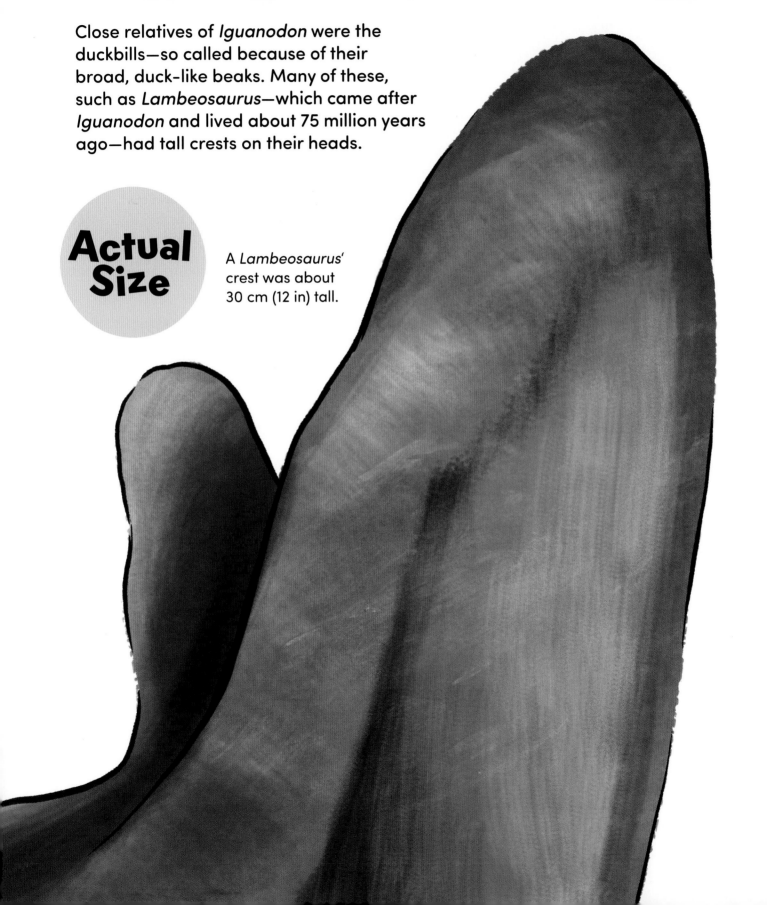

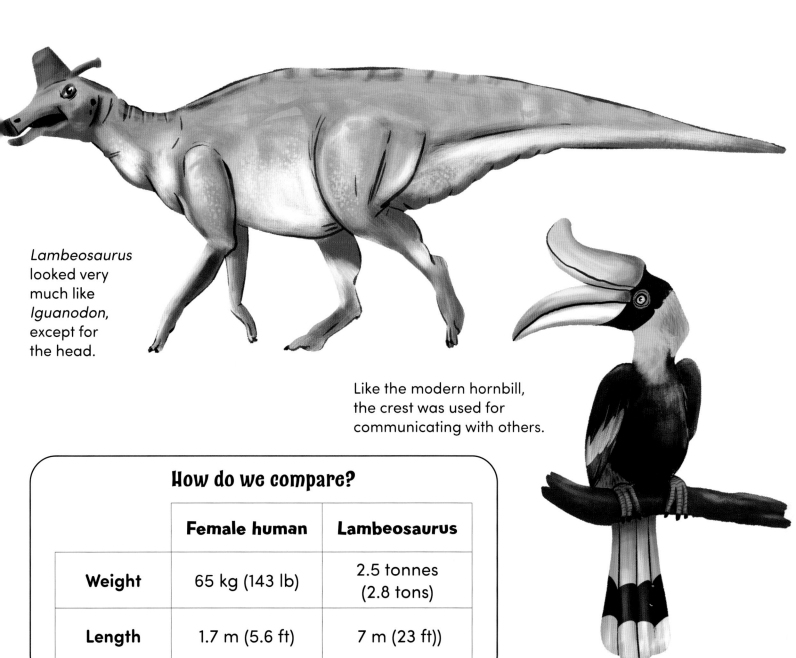

Lambeosaurus looked very much like *Iguanodon*, except for the head.

Like the modern hornbill, the crest was used for communicating with others.

How do we compare?

	Female human	Lambeosaurus
Weight	65 kg (143 lb)	2.5 tonnes (2.8 tons)
Length	1.7 m (5.6 ft)	7 m (23 ft))

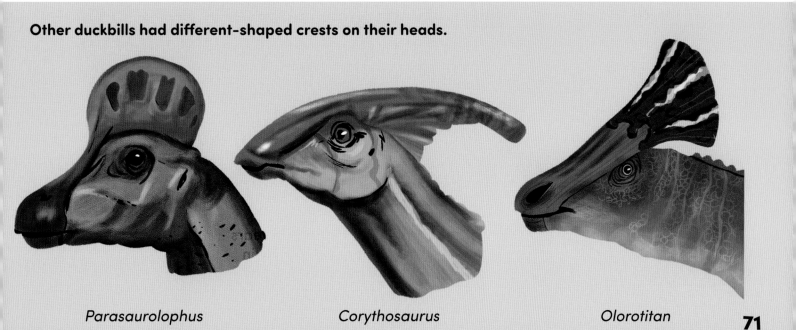

Other duckbills had different-shaped crests on their heads.

Parasaurolophus

Corythosaurus

Olorotitan

How Tough Was **Stegoceras?**

Very! *Stegoceras* belonged to the bonehead group of two-footed plant-eating dinosaurs that had massive layers of bone on the top of their heads. Sometimes these layers developed into high, solid domes. *Stegoceras* was one of these.

Actual Size

Stegoceras lived about 75 million years ago, in the Late Cretaceous period, in what is now North America.

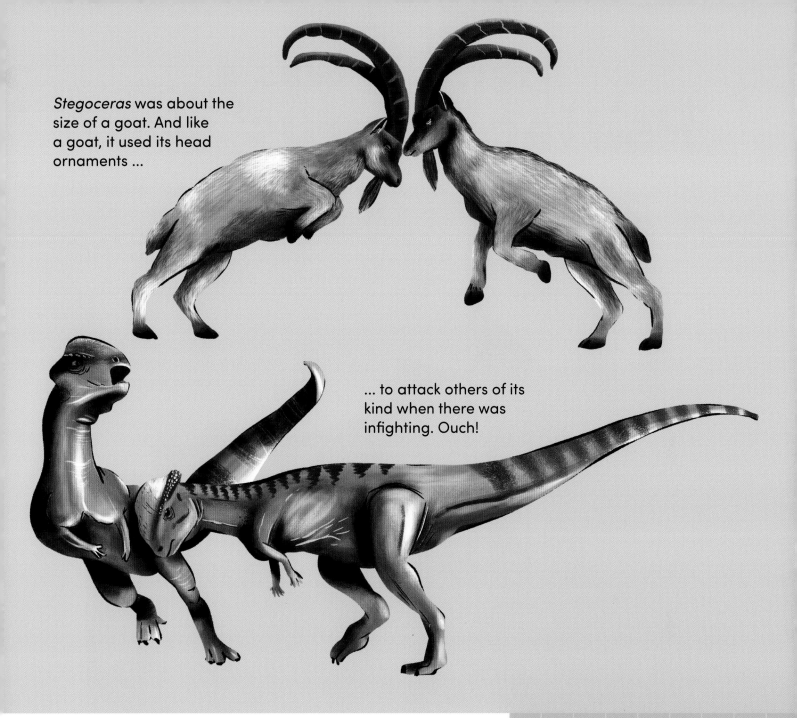

Stegoceras was about the size of a goat. And like a goat, it used its head ornaments ...

... to attack others of its kind when there was infighting. Ouch!

How do we compare?

	Female human	Stegoceras
Weight	65 kg (143 lb)	40 kg (88 lb)
Length	1.7 m (5.6 ft)	2.5 m (8.2 ft)

The biggest member of the bonehead group, *Pachycephalosaurus*, was about the size of a modern rhino.

Pachycephalosaurus

Stegoceras

How Big Was a
Psittacosaurus' Skull?

Related to the boneheads were the hornheads. One of the earlier forms was *Psittacosaurus*, which was alive about 126–100 million years ago. It was smaller than later forms, and the horns were small conical structures.

Actual Size

A *Psittacosaurus'* skull was deep, and it had a big parrot-like beak.

Psittacosaurus was the size of a small modern sheep, and it had a row of quills sticking up from its tail.

The modern parrot has a huge, strong beak it uses for breaking up seeds and other tough plant material. *Psittacosaurus* used its beak for the same purpose.

How do we compare?

	Female human	Psittacosaurus
Weight	65 kg (143 lb)	20 kg (44 lb)
Length	1.7 m (5.6 ft)	2 m (6.6 ft)

Many *Psittacosaurus* lived together, and sometimes one adult would babysit the young of the rest of the herd.

How Big Was a **Triceratops'** Horn?

Triceratops lived about 67 million years ago. It was the biggest and the last of the horned dinosaurs—so big that we can only get the tip of the horn on the page. But imagine that tip coming at you with the weight of an animal as big as a bulldozer behind it, charging at you as though you were its enemy ...

Actual Size

Triceratops in fact had three horns—"tri" means three. These were made from a substance called keratin. This is the same stuff that modern rhino horns, and your fingernails, are made from.

This hole in the neck shield of a *Triceratops* was made by the horns of a rival. Huge force would have been needed to inflict that much damage!

Triceratops lived in herds like buffalo do today. And like in buffalo herds, the males would spar with one another to see who was strong enough to lead the herd.

The body of the biggest *Triceratops* was a large as that of a modern elephant. The huge head was longer than you are.

How Big Was Repenomamus?

Mammals appeared at the same time as the dinosaurs, back in Triassic times. For most of the Age of Dinosaurs, they were all small, mouse-sized animals. But one or two were much bigger.

Fierce *Repenomamus* lived about 125 million years ago and was big and fast enough to eat baby dinosaurs.

Actual Size

Repenomamus was about the size of a modern badger. It might not sound like much, but that was big for a mammal in the Age of Dinosaurs.

Repenomamus was agile enough to raid the nests of dinosaurs and escape with their babies, which it would then eat. We know this because bones of a baby *Psittacosaurus* were found in the stomach of a *Repenomamus* fossil.

How do we compare?

	Female human	**Repenomamus**
Weight	65 kg (143 lb)	14 kg (31 lb)
Height	1.7 m (5.6 ft)	1 m (3.3 ft)

Smaller mammals of dinosaur times

Rat-sized *Cimolestes* hunted small prey.

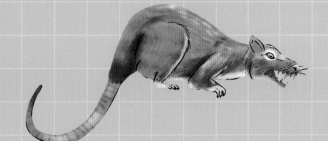

Fruitafossor was a burrowing, squirrel-sized insect-eater.

Castorocauda was a swimming mammal, like a little modern beaver.

How Big Was a
Thoatherium's Hoof?

This is the foot of a horse, isn't it? Wrong! It is the foot of a *Thoatherium,* a gazelle-like animal that 17 million years ago roamed the open grassy plains of South America, where horses never lived. So, despite what you might think, it was not related to the horse at all.

The name *Thoatherium* means "active swift-beast," and the animal's long legs do suggest that it would have been able to run fast.

Actual Size

Having a single toe with a hoof on each leg would also have helped the animal to gallop quickly across the open plains in Argentina, where fossil specimens have been found.

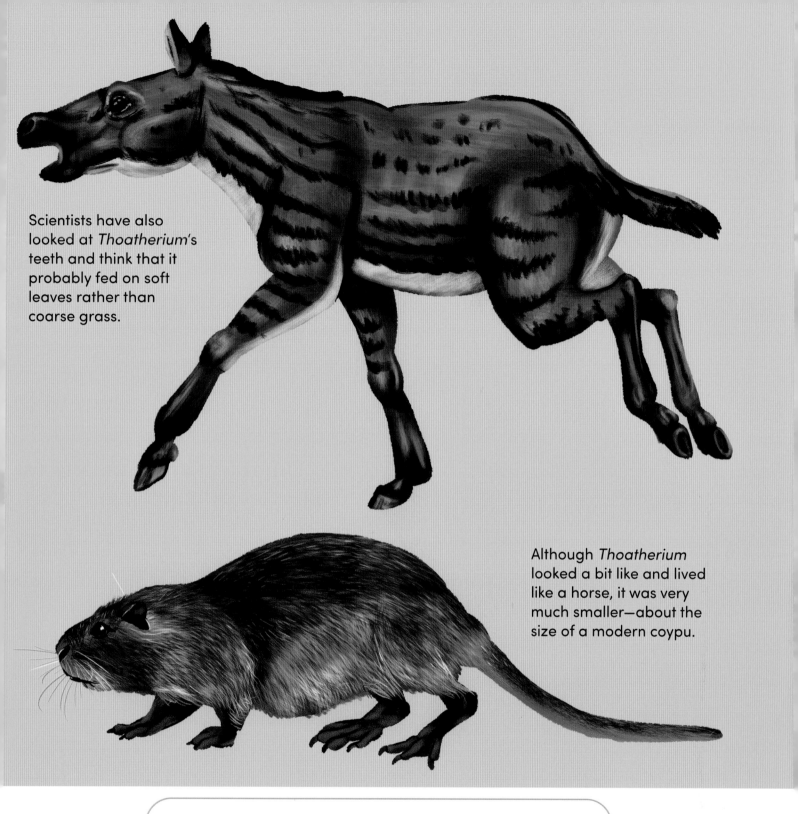

Scientists have also looked at *Thoatherium*'s teeth and think that it probably fed on soft leaves rather than coarse grass.

Although *Thoatherium* looked a bit like and lived like a horse, it was very much smaller—about the size of a modern coypu.

How do we compare?

	Female human	Thoatherium
Weight	65 kg (143 lb)	11 kg (24 lb)
Height	1.7 m (5.6 ft)	70 cm 2.3 ft

How Big Was a Chalicotherium's Claw?

This claw belonged to a relative of the horse called *Chalicotherium*, which lived 25–5 million years ago. The claw was used to bring down branches so the animal could eat the juicy leaves.

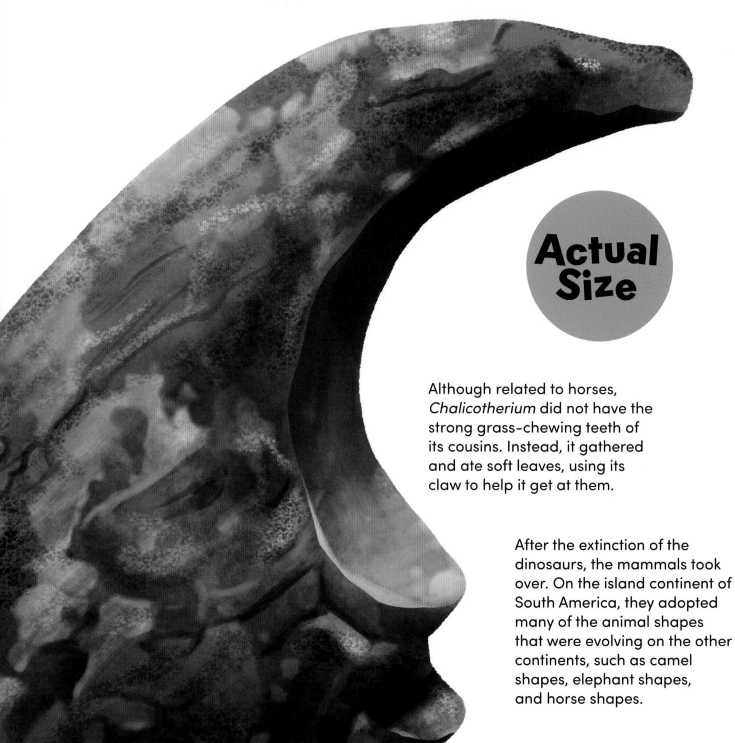

Actual Size

Although related to horses, *Chalicotherium* did not have the strong grass-chewing teeth of its cousins. Instead, it gathered and ate soft leaves, using its claw to help it get at them.

After the extinction of the dinosaurs, the mammals took over. On the island continent of South America, they adopted many of the animal shapes that were evolving on the other continents, such as camel shapes, elephant shapes, and horse shapes.

Chalicotherium was distantly related to the horse, but it was bigger than the biggest breed of carthorse that exists today.

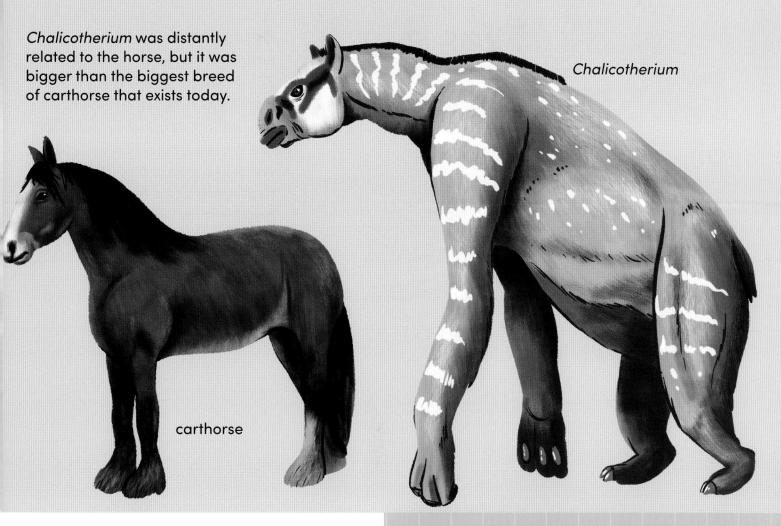

Chalicotherium

carthorse

The long front legs made *Chalicotherium* walk with a sloping back, and it could sit on its bottom at rest. It walked on its knuckles like a gorilla, so its claws would not be damaged.

Chalicotherium could stand on its strong hind legs and reach up to a height of about 4 m (13 ft) into the trees to feed on the soft leaves, stripping them from the branches with its thick lips.

How do we compare?

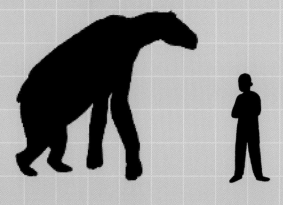

How Big Was a Desmostylus' Skull?

Desmostylus was like a walrus and lived in the sea 28–7 million years ago. It had long tusks at the front for feeling around for food in the water, and its back teeth were like packed solid pillars that were used for grinding hard things like shellfish.

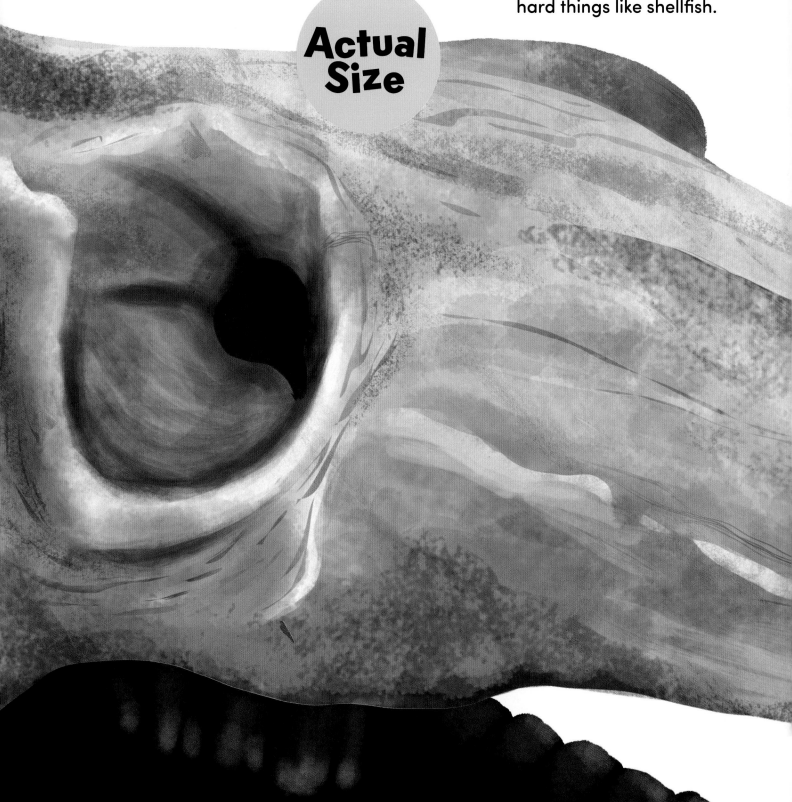

Actual Size

Like a modern walrus, *Desmostylus* lived in shallow water and used its tusks to dig up shellfish from the sea bed. However, instead of flippers, it had legs that were more useful on land. It could row itself along underwater like a modern hippopotamus.

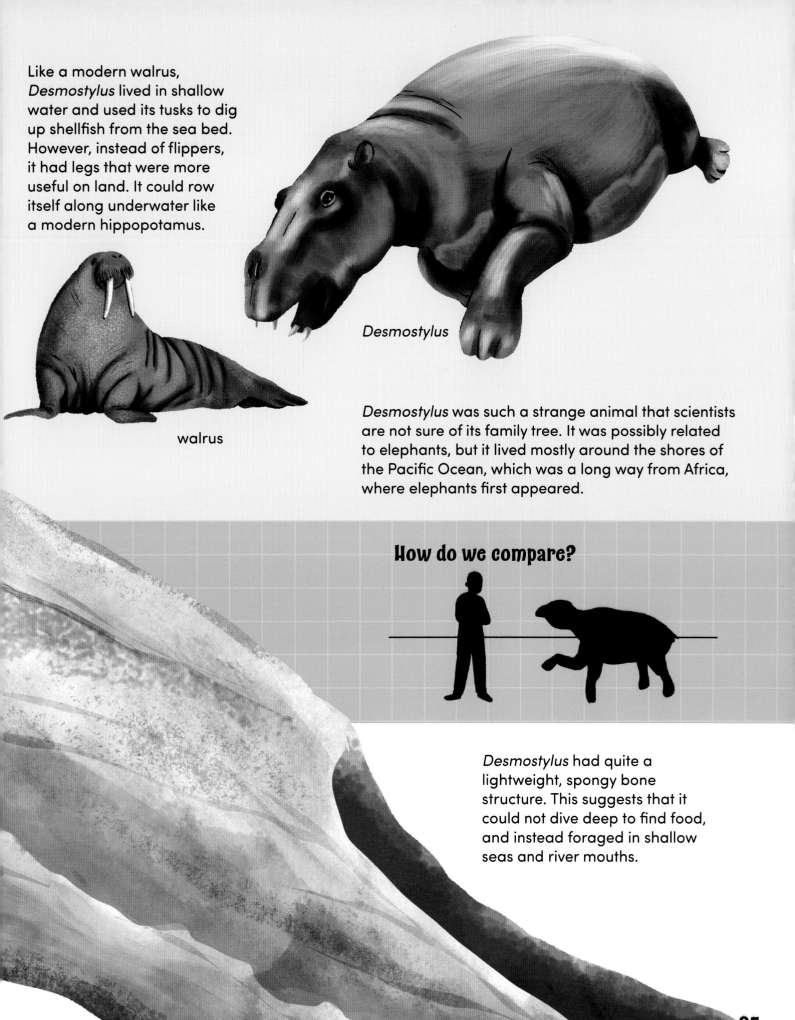

walrus

Desmostylus

Desmostylus was such a strange animal that scientists are not sure of its family tree. It was possibly related to elephants, but it lived mostly around the shores of the Pacific Ocean, which was a long way from Africa, where elephants first appeared.

How do we compare?

Desmostylus had quite a lightweight, spongy bone structure. This suggests that it could not dive deep to find food, and instead foraged in shallow seas and river mouths.

How Big Were Protocetus' Jaws?

These are the teeth of an early whale called *Protocetus* that lived during the Eocene period, about 45 million years ago. Most early whales had strong triangular teeth like these, but the rest of the animal did not look like a whale at all.

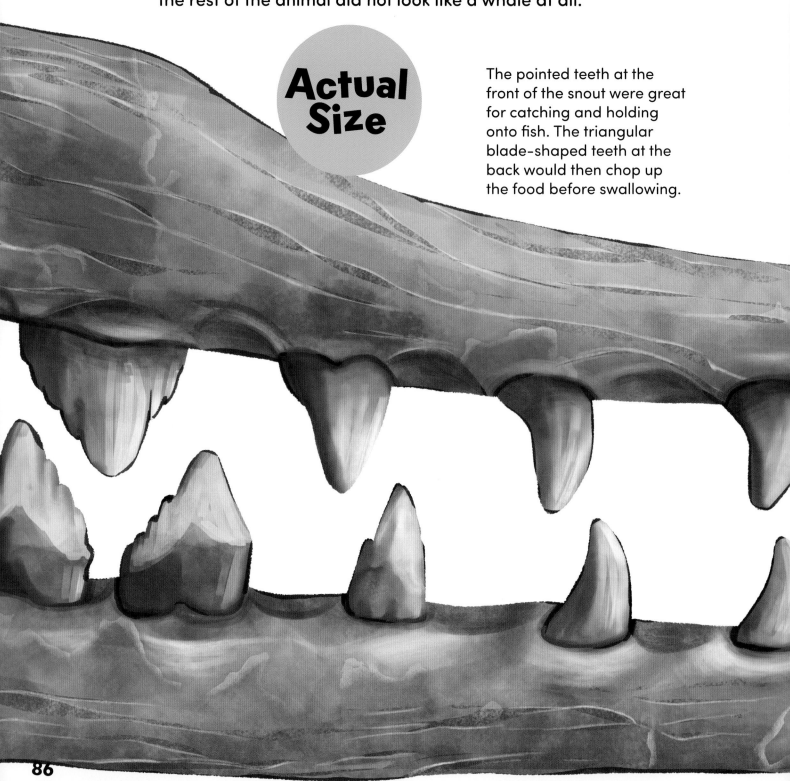

Actual Size

The pointed teeth at the front of the snout were great for catching and holding onto fish. The triangular blade-shaped teeth at the back would then chop up the food before swallowing.

Protocetus was about the size of a large dolphin, but it must have spent most of its life on land. The whales became fully aquatic little by little.

Other early whales

The first whales were fully land-living animals like modern pigs.

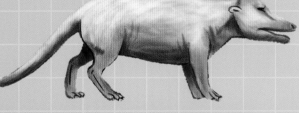

Eventually, they became semi-aquatic, like hippos.

Then more aquatic like seals.

And finally fully ocean-going, as they are today.

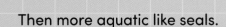

87

How Big Was a Mammoth's Tooth?

The tooth of a woolly mammoth was hard and wrinkly on its exposed side. These are grinding surfaces, which allowed the mammoth to chew the hard Arctic plants on which it fed until it became extinct about 4,000 years ago.

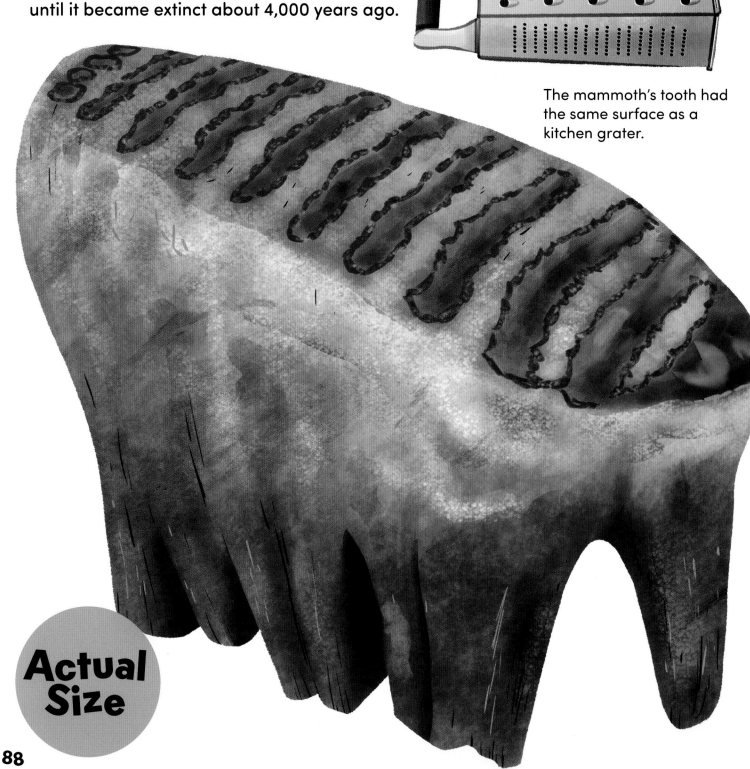

The mammoth's tooth had the same surface as a kitchen grater.

Actual Size

The great tusks of the mammoth were up to 4.2 m (14 ft) long. The animal used them as scrapers for pushing the snow away to find its food of mosses, lichens, flowering herbs, grasses, and shrubs.

We think of mammoths as being very huge. In fact, although there were very large mammoth species, it is the woolly mammoth that we are mostly familiar with, and this was only about the same size as a modern Asiatic elephant. So it was definitely big, but not massive!

The woolly mammoth had useful adaptations to protect it from the cold. Under the skin was a layer of fat that was as thick as a mattress, to keep the heat in. There were two layers of insulating fur—a short undercoat and an outer covering of longer hairs.

Our ancestors knew exactly how big the mammoth was. They saw them, hunted them, and drew them on their cave walls.

How Big Were Smilodon's Teeth?

Smilodon, the so-called "sabre-toothed tiger" (or "saber-toothed tiger"), was a fierce hunter during the Ice Age. It used its huge sword-like canine teeth to kill the big animals of the time.

Smilodon was a top predator that lived in the Americas from 2.5 million years ago right up until 10,000 years ago.

How does it compare?

Smilodon was about the same size as a modern tiger, but the two animals are not closely related.

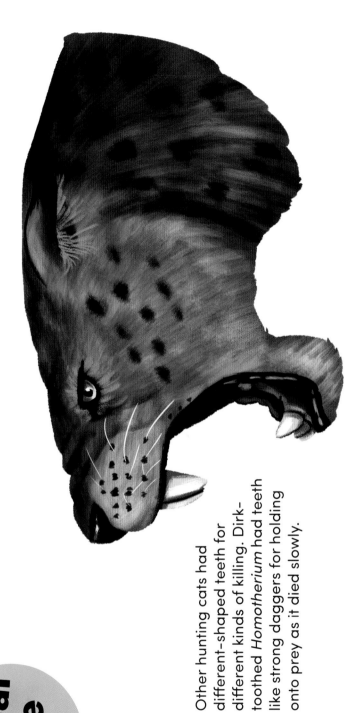

Smilodon

tiger

Smilodon features included:

- Sword-like teeth to do the killing quickly.
- Strong forelimbs to hold down struggling prey.
- A short tail. A modern tiger uses its long tail for balance as it runs.
- *Smilodon* did not chase its prey—it lunged at it from a sudden ambush.

Actual Size

Other hunting cats had different-shaped teeth for different kinds of killing. Dirk-toothed *Homotherium* had teeth like strong daggers for holding onto prey as it died slowly.

How Big Was Darwinius?

One of the best-known of the early primates—ancestors to lemurs, monkeys, apes, and ourselves—is *Darwinius*. But how big was it, and what did it look like?

Darwinius measured about 60 cm (2 ft) in length, including its long tail.

Actual Size

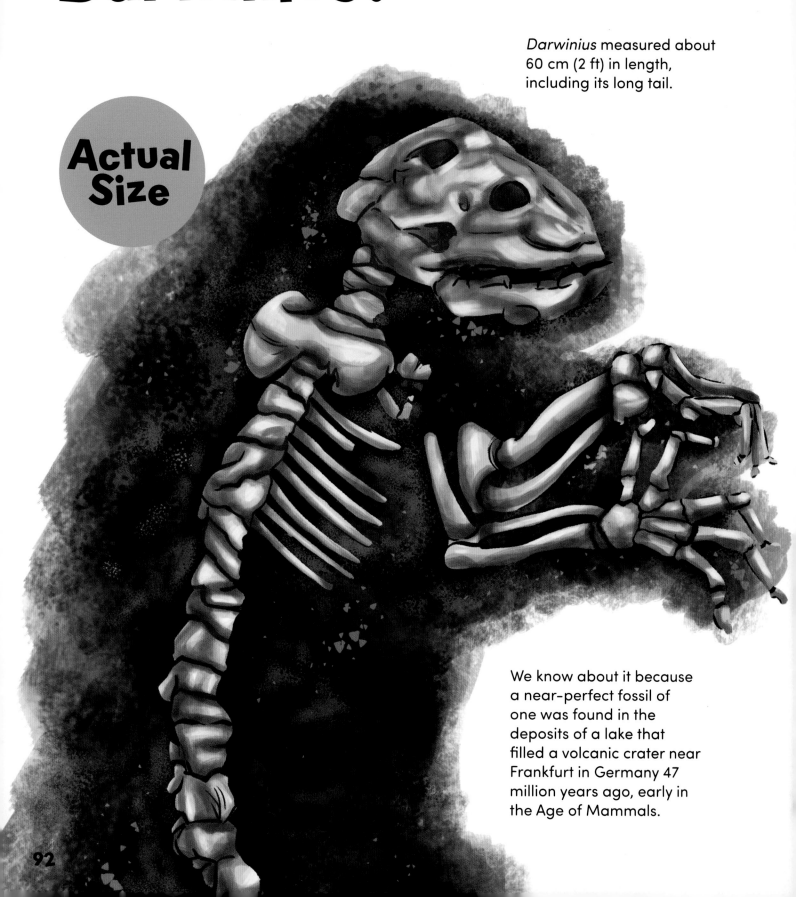

We know about it because a near-perfect fossil of one was found in the deposits of a lake that filled a volcanic crater near Frankfurt in Germany 47 million years ago, early in the Age of Mammals.

Darwinius was a small tree-living animal—about the size of a modern squirrel.

How do we compare?

	Female human	Darwinius
Weight	65 kg (143 lb)	436 kg (961 lb)
Length	1.7 m (5.6 ft)	58 cm (23 in)

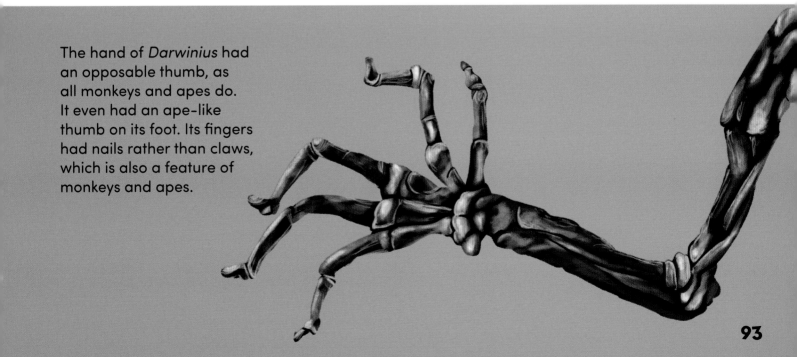

The hand of *Darwinius* had an opposable thumb, as all monkeys and apes do. It even had an ape-like thumb on its foot. Its fingers had nails rather than claws, which is also a feature of monkeys and apes.

Invertebrates

Invertebrates are divided into many different groups, including insects, arachnids, jellyfish, mollusks, squid, and gastropods. Many of them have a hard outer shell called an exoskeleton. Examples in this book: *Jaekelopterus, Arthropleura, Anomalocaris, Hallucigenia, Opabinia, Meganeura.*

Vertebrates Divided into groups, or classes, as follows:

Mammal

Warm-blooded creatures that give birth to live young and feed them with their mother's milk. They mostly have fur or hair on their bodies. Examples in this book: *Repenomamus, Thoatherium,* coypu, *Chalicotherium, Smilodon.*

Bird

Creatures that have wings, feathers, and a beak or bill. They lay eggs and many of them can fly. Birds evolved from a group of meat-eating dinosaurs called theropods. *Archaeopteryx* is believed to be the earliest bird.

Glossary

Aquatic Living in the water like a fish. Semi-aquatic means living in the water sometimes, like a modern hippopotamus does.

Arthropod Meaning "jointed limb"—a group of invertebrate animals that have hard outer coverings and jointed legs, such as insects.

Chameleon A kind of lizard that lives by clinging to tree branches, is slow-moving, can change to match its surroundings, and catches insects with a long, fast tongue.

Cheek pouch A fleshy bag-like structure at the side of the mouth for holding food while chewing.

Cold-blooded animal An animal that, unlike a warm-blooded animal, cannot adjust its body temperature. Fish, amphibians, and reptiles are cold-blooded. When the weather is hot, they become hot; when the weather is cold, they become cold.

Crest A structure on the top of an animal's head, usually for showing off to other animals.

Dirk A kind of dagger or a small sword.

Evolve For a living thing to change, from generation to generation, resulting in its offspring having different shapes or habits.

Feather A lightweight structure made of the same stuff as your hair or fingernails. It is usually branched or fluffy and is used for insulation or flying.

Fossil The remains of a once-living organism that has changed by being buried for thousands or millions of years.

Herb Any low-growing plant.

Hoof A very strong toenail that supports the weight of an animal as it walks or runs.

Horn A structure made of the same stuff as your hair or fingernails, and usually used for showing off or fighting.

Lichen A kind of low-growing plant formed of a mixture of fungi and algae that often grows in barren places where not much else survives.

Membrane A very thin sheet of living matter in a plant or an animal.

Reptile

Cold-blooded creatures that are covered in dry skin and scales. Their young hatch from eggs. Dinosaurs are reptiles. Examples of reptiles in this book: *Westlothiana, Archelon, Tyrannosaurus*, plus many others.

Amphibian

Cold-blooded creatures that have gills and lungs for breathing. Their young live in the water and move onto land as adults. Most have slimy or sticky skin. Example in this book: *Platyhystrix*.

Fish

Creatures that live in the water; they have scales, fins, and breathe through gills. Examples in this book: *Cephalaspis, Dunkleosteus*.

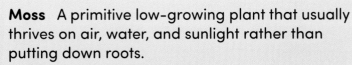

Moss A primitive low-growing plant that usually thrives on air, water, and sunlight rather than putting down roots.

Paddle A limb that has a flat shape and is used by an animal for swimming.

Predator An animal that hunts for food (known as its prey).

Prey An animal that is eaten by another animal.

Primate The group of mammals to which the monkeys, apes, and humans belong.

Pterosaur A flying reptile that existed alongside the dinosaurs. It was warm-blooded and able to fly by means of a pair of membrane wings attached to long fourth fingers.

Rookery A collection of nests where a whole flock of birds, or pterosaurs, live together.

Saber Sometimes spelled "sabre"—a kind of curved sword.

Sail In an animal—a skin-covered structure supported by bony struts growing upward from the backbone.

Scale A small plate of horny material that grows from the skin of some animals, like reptiles and fish.

Scute A very large, tough scale that forms a protective structure, like those we see on the skin of alligators.

Skeleton The bones that form the internal framework of a vertebrate.

Termite An ant-like arthropod that lives in colonies, eats woody substances, and builds hill-like nests.

Tusk A tooth that is long and strong, and usually continuously growing.

Warm-blooded animal An animal that can adjust its body temperature, so that it can keep warm in cold weather and can cool off in hot weather. A warm-blooded animal needs much more food and energy than a cold-blooded animal that does not have this ability. Mammals, birds, and some dinosaurs are examples.

Wingspan The distance from the tip of a bird or pterosaur's wing to the tip of its other wing.

Index